All rights reserved.

Copyright © 2024 Alissa .J Denton

Nurture Yourself: Best Caregiver Self-Care Tips : Revive Your Well-being: Essential Self-Care Strategies for Caregivers

Funny helpful tips:

Stay connected with health professionals; regular check-ups and consultations ensure optimal health.

Rotate between fiction and non-fiction; a balanced reading diet enriches both the mind and soul.

Nurture Yourself: Best Caregiver Self-Care Tips

Alissa .J Denton

<u>Life advices:</u>

In the river of experiences, flow with grace, learning from each twist and turn.

Your essence is a light; let it shine brightly, guiding and uplifting others.

Introduction

This is a comprehensive resource designed to support and empower caregivers on their journey. In this guide, caregivers will find practical advice and actionable strategies to prioritize their emotional, physical, and spiritual well-being while tending to the needs of their loved ones.

The emotional well-being section encourages caregivers to assess and manage their emotions effectively. It provides insights on adapting to change, expressing feelings, and building emotional intelligence. The guide emphasizes the importance of creating a supportive network by connecting with other caregivers and seeking professional help when needed. Caregivers are encouraged to embrace their new reality, manage anger, and navigate the complex emotions associated with caregiving.

For physical self-care, the guide offers valuable tips on pacing oneself, adopting healthy eating habits, staying hydrated, and incorporating physical activities like dancing, yoga, and cardio. Caregivers are reminded to pay attention to warning signs of burnout, manage fatigue, and prioritize sleep. The guide also emphasizes the significance of grooming, dressing for success, and scheduling regular medical check-ups.

The section on spiritual and soulful self-care delves into practices such as meditation, gratitude, and connecting with nature. Caregivers are encouraged to reward themselves, practice mindfulness, and find joy in small victories. The guide recognizes the temporary nature of caregiving challenges and suggests various activities, from journaling to enjoying an occasional ice cream splurge, to nourish the spirit.

The practical self-care section provides caregivers with actionable advice for managing their time efficiently, handling medical responsibilities, and building effective support teams. From tracking time and researching drug interactions to creating calming environments and dealing with legal documents, caregivers are equipped with practical tools to navigate the complexities of caregiving.

Throughout the guide, the importance of communication, setting boundaries, and asking for help is emphasized. Caregivers are encouraged to celebrate their resilience, stay connected with their spirituality, and approach each day with a positive mindset. By incorporating the strategies outlined in this guide, caregivers can cultivate a holistic approach to self-care, fostering resilience, and maintaining their well-being as they navigate the challenges of caregiving.

Contents

Chapter 1: Self-Care for Your Emotions 1
Take Your Emotional Temperature 3
Let Mistakes Be Teachers 4
Embrace Your New Life Even When You Resent the Loss of Your Old One 5
Give Yourself Time to Adjust 7
Daydream to Unwind 9
Rid Yourself of the Downers 11
Adapt to Change 13
Have a Good Cry 15
Talk to Other Caregivers 16
Create a Sanctuary 17
Take It Easy 18
Don't Make Decisions after Dark 19
Express Your Feelings Instead of Stuffing Them 20
Develop Your Emotional Intelligence 21
Accept the Things You Cannot Change 23
Regain Your Tolerance 25
Listen to Your Heart 27
Make Coming Unglued a Good Experience 28
Look Back, but Don't Stare 29
Be a Self-Aware Caregiver 31
Be Spontaneous 33
Choose Happiness over Being Right 34
Accept the Big Feelings Caregiving Triggers 35

Give Up the Ghosts 36
Seek Professional Help 37
Escape Emotional Traps 38
Manage Your Anger 39
Acknowledge Grief 40
Face Your Fear 41
Deal With the Caregiver Blues 43
Manage Your Worry 45
Understand That It's Okay to Not Be Okay 46
Avoid Perfectionism 47
Get Rid of the Guilt 48
Trust Yourself 49
Chapter 2: Self-Care for Your Body 50
Pace Yourself 53
Think of Yourself As an Athlete 54
Eat Like a Champion 55
Dance 57
Dress for Success 58
Hydrate 59
Don't Skip Meals—Snack 61
Keep Up with Your Grooming 62
Make Doctors' Appointments for Yourself 65
Manage Fatigue and Sleep Deprivation 67
Go to the Bathroom 68
Look for Warning Signs of Caregiver Burnout 69
Pay Attention to Your Headache 71
Train Your Brain 72

Get Out in Nature 73

Book a Massage 74

Tune In to Your Body 75

Avoid Drugs and Excessive Alcohol 76

Limit Caffeine 77

Invest In the Perfect Shoes 78

Take Your Vitamins 79

Do Cardio! 80

Indulge In Facials 81

Pamper Your Gut 82

Practice Yoga 83

Hire Someone to Help 84

Breathe for Balance 85

Use Sleep As a Weapon 87

Create a Caregiver's Spa 89

Savor Your Meals 91

Moisturize 93

Practice Mindfulness with the Five Senses 94

Watch Out for Exertion/Exhaustion 95

Use Grounding Techniques to Alleviate Anxiety 97

Chapter 3: Self-Care for Your Spirit and Soul 98

Meditate 101

Don't Do It Alone 102

Reward Yourself Once a Day 103

Honor and Respect Others 104

Be Grateful 105

Remember This Is Temporary 107

Pet Your Pet	108
Journal about Caregiving	109
Manage Your Time on Social Media	111
Give Yourself a Parade	113
Pick Your Battles	114
Play Your Favorite Music and Sing	115
Sit in the Sun	116
Live Just for Today	117
Enjoy an Occasional Ice Cream Splurge	118
Go Float Your Boat	119
Establish an End-of-Day Ritual	120
Hit the Restart Button	121
Be Kind to Yourself	122
Celebrate Small Victories	123
Stop Worrying about What Others Think	124
Let Go of Control	125
Get Rid of the Judge in Your Head	127
Laugh!	129
Begin Your Day Expecting Miracles	131
Zip Your Lips	132
Regain Your Balance	133
Stay In Touch with Your Spirituality	135
Listen to Your Heart	136
Communicate with the Family	137
Set Boundaries	139
Learn When to Lean In or Back Off	141
Say What You Mean, Mean What You Say, but Don't Say It Mean	143

Ask for Help 145
Let Empathy Guide You 147
Chapter 4: Practical Self-Care 148
Track Your Time 151
Pause Between Reaction and Action 152
Be Willing to Learn 153
Research Drug Interactions and Side Effects 155
Get the Donkey Out of the Ditch 156
Work Smarter, Not Harder 157
Keep Up with the Spinning Plates 159
Keep an Updated Contact List 160
Manage Meds Effectively 161
Don't Assume 163
Put One Foot in Front of the Other 164
Get the Most Out of Doctors' Visits 165
Keep a "Go Bag" of Essentials by the Front Door 167
Do One Task at a Time 169
Keep Moving 170
Create Effective To-Do Lists 171
Take the Action, Then Let Go of the Results 172
Just Move the Needle 173
Deal With Distraction 174
Schedule Like a Pro 175
Create a Calming Environment 177
Stick to Your Rituals 178
Establish Great Relationships 179
Get an Action Partner 181

Build a Team 182
Create a Budget 183
Wait Twenty-Four Hours 184
Sleep On It 185
Know Your Limitations 186
Listen and Win 187
Stop Isolation by Socializing 188
Handle Legal Documents 189
Don't Argue, Don't Correct 191

Manage a Crisis 193
Deal With the Aftereffects of a Crisis 195

Chapter 1: Self-Care for Your Emotions

Caregiving can be an emotional roller coaster ride, bringing big, surprising, and sometimes debilitating feelings to the surface. Every caregiver is unique, and the emotional reactions you will experience are as individual as you are, but all caregivers have one thing in common: You will be affected emotionally in ways that will change your life forever.

Emotional self-care is vital to staying ahead of the emotional curveballs caregiving can throw into your life. Knowing how to manage the emotional toll of caregiving and its aftermath is critical to being your healthiest and best self. In this chapter, you will find simple yet powerful activities and actions you can take to insulate, protect, and heal yourself from the big emotions caregiving can bring about. These activities will inspire you to prioritize your self-care and to remember that your feelings and emotions matter and that you are entitled to having them, understanding them, sitting with them, and coming up with the best possible way to manage them for the healthiest and most effective outcome.

Your emotions are your guidelines. They are important indicators of how caregiving is affecting you and how you need to move forward to stay balanced and flourish. This chapter will give you tools for emotional awareness and stability that every caregiver needs to thrive.

Take Your Emotional Temperature

As a caregiver, it is critical that you stop for a moment and check in with your feelings. What are you feeling right now? Are you frustrated, angry, scared, worried? You so generously worry about the feelings of others, now is the time for you to acknowledge your own.

By taking an emotional "time-out" to check in with your feelings, you have a chance to experience them instead of letting them build up. You can't make your feelings disappear, but by being aware of them, they lose their power, giving you a chance to feel them and then let them go. The only way to get over feelings is to go through them.

Sit still and feel what's going on. Tell yourself it's okay to feel whatever it is you are feeling. Anger, frustration, fear, and guilt are common and normal reactions during the caregiving journey. Give yourself permission to feel these emotions. Caregiving can be hard and upsetting. Tell yourself that, while it may feel uncomfortable right now, you are going to feel your painful emotions instead of stuffing them down inside. Remember that there is nothing wrong with feeling angry or afraid or sad. Should you feel consumed with the emotions you are feeling and they seem overwhelming, it may be time to seek help from your doctor or therapist. There is no reason to be ashamed or afraid to reach out to others when big feelings are triggered. You are not alone.

Let Mistakes Be Teachers

Mistakes are good things if you use them as teachers and learn from them. It is not always easy to take this positive, mature, and balanced view, especially during the caregiving journey, when the stakes feel so high and consequences feel larger than life.

Yet, we are human, and we all make mistakes. Caregiving is one of the most likely fields for mistakes to happen because the territory is often unexpected and unknown. You can rarely handle everything you confront without a stumble here and there. Try these tools when you make a mistake:

- Frame the mistake this way: You have learned something. You'll never do that thing that way ever again. You now know better. Accept the responsibility for the mistake so you can make it your friend.
- Ask yourself: "What happened, why did it happen, what's my part, what went wrong, what was learned about the situation and myself?" Write down the answers.
- Look over your answers and see if there is anything you can do right now to prevent the same type of situation from happening again.
- Write down any actions you can take to give you an edge when a similar situation arises.
- Forgive yourself. Remember, you are serving others; you have the best intentions, and you are a good person. Now you are smarter. Don't wallow; instead, wonder and be thankful for the wisdom.

Embrace Your New Life Even When You Resent the Loss of Your Old One

Any way you look at it, once you step into the caregiver role, your life is changed forever. You are now completely focused on the needs of others, committed to doing everything you can to ensure that those you care for are safe, comfortable, and pain-free. You are prioritizing their lives, and to do that you need to make concessions with yours.

This can be frustrating and upsetting when you feel that your life as you knew it is gone and things seem so different. It may seem as though you have permanently lost your old life in exchange for a new one. You can become resentful as time passes and you begin to miss the things you used to do and the time and energy you had to do them. It's hard to ease the pain and frustration you feel when you can't be as free and self-concerned as you are used to being. You most certainly are entitled to be a little grouchy and sad about the changes in your life. You are mourning what feels like the loss of your identity and lifestyle. You may even feel lost.

Although it is completely understandable to have these thoughts and feelings, you need to keep things in perspective. You need to remind yourself that this new normal is not forever. It's just for today. Even though your todays may be creating a chain of weeks and years, you can only know what the present brings. Projecting into a future you know nothing about is a waste of time and energy. You have no idea what will happen tomorrow and where your life or the lives of those you protect will be then. It could all change so quickly, and everything would be different yet again.

So focus on what is happening today. As difficult and exhausting as caregiving can be, it is an honor to care for those who cared for you or those you have chosen to serve. You do so out of a need and desire to provide love and attention to those who need it the most. The sense of satisfaction and fulfillment in carrying out this special mission is like no other. Even with the temporary loss of your old normal and the life you knew, the payoff and gratification are undeniable. Where would you be without these wonderful people in your life, and how lucky are you to have this chance to give back to them what they so generously gave you and the world?

By embracing every little smile and sweet thank you, and seeing that you have made such a difference in someone else's life, you may find that the changes to your own life become less important.

You will return to your old life at some point. When you do, it will be a more complete, richer life than it was before.

Give Yourself Time to Adjust

If you were starting a new job, moving to a new town, or dating someone new, you would know you need time to adjust. By allowing yourself an adjustment period as you begin a caregiving role, you let everyone (including those you care for) have time to settle in.

Most caregivers have little time to prepare for their new role of caregiving. A family emergency, a sudden illness, or a serious injury forces someone to step up to the caregiver role. Circumstances like this demand that new caregivers jump in and hit the ground running. There usually is an immediacy to the situation that can be daunting.

Although there is so much to do and understand and because there might be an immediate crisis to deal with, you must remember to give yourself and your loved ones time to adjust. The knee-jerk reaction of wanting to fix everything right away is not only unrealistic; it's also risky. Stress can build up quickly if you try to do too much too fast. It's best to ease into the new role.

You can avoid trouble by being aware of your need to be all things to all people. Be on the lookout for any sign that you feel an intense need or pressure to fix those you care for and any issues they may have. You are not responsible for fixing anything. What you are responsible for is showing up and supporting those you serve and ensuring that the best care is available to them.

While you may need to resolve big and important issues, and the expectations of others may cause you concern, the reality is that nothing changes instantly, and the way to resolve these issues is to keep things simple, tackling what you can, when you can, as calmly as possible.

When you feel yourself wanting to do all of it at once, remember you are in a period of observation and change. You need a moment to take it all in, to figure it all out, and to see how it all feels. This adjustment period should take however long you need it to. Most caregivers are in an adjustment period the entire time they are caregivers! Things are always in flux. Give yourself space to adapt and adjust.

In the early days of caregiving, just start by showing up. Listen, watch, read the room and take it all in. Remember that you might not know everything just yet. Take the time to see how everyone is feeling and be open and curious. Learn the ropes. Take it easy, breathe, pause, and reflect. Let it unfold and know that more will be revealed.

Daydream to Unwind

Imagination plays such an important role in caregiving. How you make decisions and face change during your caregiving journey has so much to do with the connections and calculations your powerful brain makes. So much is going on up there that you are not even aware of! Behind the scenes, your imagination is processing pros and cons so that eventually you can come up with solutions and answers.

You can use that imagination to help yourself daydream. Daydreaming is a getaway ticket to a place where you can be free of worry and concern about those you care for, change your outlook, and recharge.

Daydreaming relaxes your body and your mind, and it can have a positive effect on your mood and general well-being. If you organize some space and time to allow yourself some much-needed daydreaming, you can reap the benefits and be even more focused afterward.

It's important to be in the right frame of mind to enjoy and get the most out of daydreaming. If you are going down a rabbit hole worrying and ruminating about negative things, it's not the right time to daydream. But if you could use a break from the normal caregiving hustle and bustle and you can allow yourself to put your mind to work for you to visualize and fantasize about fun and happiness, the results can be rewarding.

Of course, there is a time and place for daydreaming. You shouldn't use daydreaming to avoid what needs to be done or to put off decisions and actions you need to take. But it can be a terrific emotional vacation. Here are two helpful keys to unlocking the pleasure of a lovely daydreaming session:

1. **Pick a time to daydream.** Be specific. Plan time to take a few minutes to let your mind off the hook and just dance around pleasant thoughts and visualize happy places and things. Call this your daydream time. For those of you who worry about how long it might take, you can time this activity.

2. **Make a daydream list.** Come up with a list of happy places, thoughts, and future outcomes you can daydream about. Write them down in a notebook or journal. Pick one or two for each session. Each item on your list will be a place you can travel to that becomes familiar and more vivid and entertaining each time you visit or create it.

Add daydreaming to your caregiver self-care routine and practice it consistently to entertain your mind, body, and soul. Take flight and put all your cares behind you for a few minutes. You deserve this special time!

Rid Yourself of the Downers

We all have them in our lives, those people whose glass is always half empty, and no matter how great something is they can find something wrong with it—they are the downers. Nothing is ever good enough, life is full of woe and doom and gloom, and there's no end in sight of negative things headed our way. If you're a caregiver, these are the people you don't need around you. Caregiving is hard enough without the negative attitudes of others dragging you down.

Even though you may love this person dearly, for your own well-being you may need to limit your exposure to them or remove them from your life. This may not be an easy conversation, but be truthful about how you feel. If you have the time and energy, have a gentle conversation with this person and tell them you need to be surrounded by upbeat, positive energy, and their negativity is unpleasant. While this may be upsetting to them, it will help you set boundaries, and they may hear you and try to be less of a downer.

As a caregiver you should try to surround yourself with positive, supportive people you trust. Socialization is so important to caregivers and is a great source of affirming feedback. Hang out with people who make you feel good. Make a list of the people you feel happy and safe with. These are the people you need to spend your precious social time with. Caregiving is challenging enough without having to listen to someone who is always putting a negative spin on everything.

Distance yourself from the downers. Reduce the time you spend with them. You are not obligated to hang out with or communicate with anyone. You'll feel better, and they may get the hint.

If you do have to be with the downer, try to do so in a group setting. This can save you from being the target of the negativity, and you won't be exposed to as much of it since other people are added to the mix. If you are stuck with a downer because you work with them or they are a family member, keep the conversation short or upbeat and steer it in a direction that is not triggering for you or encouraging them. Don't let their negativity rule the conversation.

Excuse yourself from their presence, walk away from the conversation if need be, and try to remember that you don't have to share their beliefs or be influenced by their behavior.

Adapt to Change

Caregivers often have valid reasons to maintain a schedule and stick to routines, especially when caring for people with Alzheimer's or dementia, or anyone with cognitive issues, who can be thrown off and frightened by change. Staying on course during the day can make the difference between successfully hitting all the marks and getting everything done or falling seriously behind. When you start to change things around, any situation can feel uncontrollable.

This is true about change in general. Change is unsettling because it shakes things up. Even if how you are doing something is not the best way to do it or how you are being is not the best way to be, it's familiar and unthreatening. Even little changes can feel uncomfortable, and you might try to avoid them at all costs. Change can feel like an excruciating setback when you are caregiving.

However, change is the one consistent thing about life. Nowhere is change more apparent than in the lives of caregivers. If you are rigid and unbending about making and embracing change, it can break you.

Learning to cope with change is a critical step toward a more balanced and relaxed caregiver journey. It takes commitment and desire to accept things and situations that are new and different. You can begin by understanding the need to make change your friend and be open to the possibilities it can bring you. Once you can get used to accepting and surrendering to the unknown and unfamiliar, you can even welcome and look forward to it!

Here are a few tactics to meet the challenge of change in a more welcoming, positive way:

- When things change, you fear you will lose something—that things will never be the same. This is a legitimate concern. Be kind to yourself about being worried. You are not alone. There are caregivers out there feeling the same thing.

- Remind yourself that things always change, and most times for the better. This change might make things easier.
- Talk it out. Don't hold back on reaching out and sharing your concerns with someone else, especially if they have been through a similar situation or are caring for someone. Chances are you'll get some great advice and support.
- Think about the change and how it affects you. Weigh the pros and cons. Write them down. The cons will be easy, but the pros are where the magic is. Think about the possibilities that this change holds. This change may be foreign, but could it be exciting and refreshing?
- Accept the fact that although change feels like you are losing control over what's happening next, you really don't have control over anything. Life is fluid, ever-changing, and something you have no control over.

Just because something feels new and strange doesn't mean it's bad. Time passing will help you with that. Soon it won't feel new at all.

Have a Good Cry

There comes a point in every caregiver's life when you run smack up against the wall of exhaustion and frustration. You just can't take one more thing that needs to get fixed, make another call, answer another important demand, clean up another accident, or have one more negotiating conversation. It's all too much.

Sometimes you may just burst into tears. And that is fine. It is a normal, healthy response, and we all do it. It turns out that crying can also be a helpful, positive release of emotion.

For some silly reason, caregivers sometimes believe that having a good cry is a sign of weakness, or isn't allowed, or doesn't help anything. The truth is, anything that doesn't hurt you or others and gives you relief from the caregiver dismay and exhaustion is completely permissible. It's when you permit yourself to break down that you can build yourself back up.

A deep, heartfelt cry is cathartic and is thought to have positive physical effects. A good cry gives you a minute to feel and acknowledge that you are overwhelmed, and it allows you a chance to express all the emotions that have built up from caregiving.

So don't avoid having a really good cry anytime if you feel it coming on. Let it happen, lean in to it, and know that hundreds of other caregivers have healed from a good cry. Crying it out can clear a caregiver's soul.

Talk to Other Caregivers

While it's important to reach out to get support, share stories, or ask for help from family and friends, nothing beats talking to another caregiver. No one can relate to the challenges, feelings, and concerns of caregiving better than another caregiver who has been through similar situations. They can validate the trials and tribulations, joys, and victories because they have gone through them too.

Sharing war stories and comparing notes with another caregiver can be reassuring. It's like belonging to a special club. Having someone completely relate to what you are sharing and then be able to offer their experience, strength, and hope is a real game changer.

Establish a relationship with caregivers you know and set up a regular time to catch up and share what's going on. You might even time these exchanges so you each get an allotted time to share or vent and then get feedback. Structure or timing aside, just make sure you schedule these meetings, Zoom calls, or phone calls and don't miss them no matter what is going on.

Make a list of available caregiver buddies you can turn to in times of crisis and always return the favor when they are in need. It's through sharing our stories that we see we are not alone.

Create a Sanctuary

Every caregiver needs a quiet, calming, serene place to retreat to. Having a place to sit alone with no disturbances to take a few deep breaths and regroup can make a world of difference, especially in caregiving environments where peace and quiet are lacking.

This space should automatically calm you down and offer respite. While it doesn't need to be fancy, the more you can tailor your space with surroundings that inspire you to relax and reconnect with yourself, the more effective it will be.

It can be anything from a bench outside by a tree to the bathroom behind a closed door. The most important aspect of creating this space is that you use it. Carving out time to sit away from the frenzy of caregiving is nonnegotiable. Let everyone know this is your sanctuary and you are not to be disturbed once you retreat there. Once you make a habit of claiming some time in this space, everyone in your caregiving world will learn to respect your break. Consider it a positive time-out.

Having a quiet space and using it is as important as making sure your loved ones take their necessary medications. Just like you would never let them miss their daily dosages, you must never let yourself miss taking a few moments to sit in your quiet, safe place.

Take It Easy

Many caregivers need to be taught to slow it down and take it easy. You are usually trying to beat the clock, get things done, prevent a catastrophe, or deal with a crisis. Not the types of things that usually lead to relaxation.

There is immense value, however, in being able to step back, check out yourself and the world around you for a minute, and see if you are pushing too hard or going too fast. Even though you want the best for those you care for and yourself, it may be time to back off a bit and take it easy.

As a caregiver, you probably apply this principle every day to those you care for and love, but you may find it hard to apply it to your own life. The next time you feel tense, out of breath, and like you are racing down a steep hill, picture how you might carefully and slowly help your loved one out of the tub or a chair. You would be gentle, slow, and easy. Now picture the task or day before you, take a deep breath, and see if you can slow down and apply that same gentleness and ease to yourself and how you handle things around you. With practice, taking it easy can work as well for you as it does for those you serve.

Don't Make Decisions after Dark

There is a time and place for making decisions, and how you manage this obligation as a caregiver is critical to reducing the negative effect of so much responsibility. As a rule, unless you are in crisis or you are on an important deadline, you should never make decisions at night.

When the sun goes down, treat yourself to the luxury of waiting until it comes up again to decide anything. You had a day filled with hundreds of things you need to process, and as darkness approaches and the day is ending, you are exhausted and spent, so your ability to see things clearly is greatly reduced. Use the following simple, symbolic gesture to help you put your concerns "to bed" so you don't have to face them until tomorrow.

Take a small box like a tissue box or any small container and label it your "decision box" or "God box" or something that represents a safe place to put your concern, worry, or issue. As soon as it gets dark, write down the issue that needs attention, put it in the box, and then do everything you can to let it go and forget about it. Know you can retrieve it in the morning and that it will be so much easier to solve then. Then get a good night's sleep.

Express Your Feelings Instead of Stuffing Them

Caregiving is an intense experience that brings up many big feelings like anger, fear, guilt, sadness, and joy. Resolving all the complex and sometimes startling emotions can often be just as complicated as the caregiving itself.

Your first tendency may be to stuff down your feelings, since taking the time to acknowledge and manage them seems wasteful and unimportant. The truth is, stuffing your feelings is dangerous and destructive. They will fester and grow, negatively contaminating everything you think and do. They can work against you if you don't process them.

The answer is to open up to other caregivers, trusted family and friends, and your tribe. Tell them what is going on and let them know what you are feeling. Be honest. These are people who love you and are concerned for you. They already know the tremendous pressure you are under as a caregiver because they watch you every day. They want to help in any way they can. They will be relieved to hear you out and protect and support you.

Do not hesitate to seek help from professionals if you are feeling completely overwhelmed. There is nothing wrong with seeking help to process your emotions and no shame in needing support. You deserve to feel as whole as you can during the caregiving experience. If you need motivation to ask for help, then do so for those you care for. They are the first ones who want you to feel better.

Develop Your Emotional Intelligence

Caregivers are often very emotionally intelligent people. Emotional intelligence is what gives us the ability to understand, use, and manage our emotions in a positive way so that we can be great communicators and handle conflict effectively. Caregiving channels emotional intelligence, and the more you lean on it, the more effective you become at displaying it.

The term "emotional intelligence" has been around since the 1960s and was popularized in the 1990s by author and psychologist Daniel Goleman. Your emotional intelligence helps you successfully navigate your relationships. Working on improving your emotional intelligence in the following areas can benefit every relationship you have, especially with those under your care.

- **Be empathetic.** Be open to the feelings and concerns of others. Remember that everyone is fighting some sort of battle, and this makes them who they are and dictates how they act in the world. While empathy usually comes naturally to caregivers, paying close attention to how others are acting and responding, and trying to imagine what they are going through, develops compassion. When we empathize, we harmonize.
- **Learn to be a good listener.** You can find out so much about someone if you listen to them. Everyone wants to be heard. Your loved ones don't always have to directly communicate their feelings, especially if they are physically or mentally unable to verbalize them. Their actions and behaviors may be telling you something. Think about the meaning and reasons behind even the upsetting reactions people have. They are trying to communicate their feelings to you.
- **Be self -aware.** Pay attention to your responses and feelings. If you have a strong reaction, try to figure out what brought that reaction on. Lean in to the feeling by asking yourself what it reminds you of, or why you feel the way you do. Is there something in your past this reminds you of?

Understanding the "what" and "why" behind your triggers makes it easier to resolve these issues and grow as a caregiver. Paying attention to what is going on inside you helps you understand what's going on with others.

When you positively manage your own emotions, you open the door to navigating the emotions of others. Emotional intelligence is something you can use in every interaction you have with those you serve and those who help you serve. Great relationships give you a rock-solid foundation on which you can build a dynamic caregiving experience. Developing your emotional intelligence helps you establish those great relationships.

Accept the Things You Cannot Change

Caregivers are always trying to fix everything. They set themselves up to be champions of those who need help and support. They consider this part of their caregiver job description and do everything they can to provide protection and comfort to those in their care.

This noble attitude, however, can set you up for disappointment and heartbreak because you can't always fix everything. There will be times when things will not be okay in your caregiving world, no matter what you do. You may try forcing solutions, running in circles, denying the facts, and wasting time and energy by putting extraordinary pressure on yourself to come up with unrealistic and ineffective solutions. You may fight to hold on to what you think *should* be rather than accepting what is.

It's times like these that you need acceptance. Acceptance opens the door to letting yourself off the hook to do what you can with what you have. Once you accept what is, you can work with it. Don't avoid the truth. During a challenge or situation that's scary or painful, watch how you are reacting. Are you blaming the universe or your luck, or are you wondering why you and your loved ones are singled out? It's natural to be upset and angry, but you still need to look at the reality of what is happening as opposed to resenting the fact that it is happening. Take the time to shake your fist at the sky and be mad, but once that passes, it's time to accept what is happening.

First, breathe deeply and clear your mind. Ask yourself what you need to do to be open to what's going on. See if you can look at the situation without the drama and be more objective. Ask yourself how you can move forward and do what's best for those you care for and yourself.

Then get a second opinion. Pick up the phone and run the situation by a trusted ally as well as your reactions to it. This lets you air your frustration, anger, and fear, and allows you to hear your dilemma described out loud and clarifies and defines it.

Remember, it's okay to come apart a little. Things that happen to those in your care can be scary and painful. Don't be afraid of having big emotions. Things can change quickly in the caregiver's world and throw you off balance. To get your balance back it's important to not run from the big emotions. Cry, scream, rant. The release of emotions will help you feel refreshed and ready to face the challenge.

Accepting the things you cannot change is the perfect way to cope with them. Once you stop pushing against them, you can learn to live with them.

Regain Your Tolerance

Caregivers are usually tolerant people. Their selflessness and desire to serve makes them sympathetic to the needs and wants of others. Caregivers have a positive tendency to accept others as they are and are often forgiving and understanding people. No one has more capacity for patience and tolerance than people who care for others.

This capacity may be stretched to its limits, however, by the conditions and circumstances you face during your caregiving journey. Physical pain and ailments, cognitive decline, and medical crises can affect the moods and emotions of those you care for, and the result can make it challenging to remain tolerant and kind. Aggressive or negative behavior is never easy to handle, and patients can become hard to deal with or uncomfortable to be around. When faced with difficult, angry, or mean behavior, your tolerance threshold can take a hit, and you can become grouchy and less patient.

When your tolerance has been stretched thin, try following a few simple techniques.

- **HALT and do something about it.** It's important to stop and acknowledge that you are reacting instead of responding and that your ability to be calm and balanced has slipped away. If you feel irritated or annoyed, it's time to pause and look at what's happening. What's going on with you? Is there an issue that needs to be addressed? Are you H (hungry), A (angry), L (lonely), or T (tired)? If so, HALT, grab a healthy snack, take a break, work through your anger, call a friend, or take a rest.
- **Step back and observe your loved ones from a different perspective.** It's important to spend some time trying to figure out why they are being difficult. Is there an explanation for the change in behavior or physical status in your loved ones? Are they in pain? Is something upsetting or frightening them? It's always easier to be tolerant when you understand

what's creating unusual or uncomfortable behaviors. Investigating the source of irritating or irrational behavior and getting answers switches your focus to relieving the pain, addressing the fear or discomfort, and fixing the issue as opposed to being upset by it.

- **Don't blame yourself.** When you are feeling overwhelmed or exhausted, it's tough to be patient and accommodating. This happens to all caregivers—it's just a side effect of caregiving, and it will pass. Be kind and patient with yourself. This is merely a bump in the road.

Tolerance never disappears; it just hides behind the clouds sometimes. Take it easy, and, like the sun, tolerance will shine on you and your loved ones once again.

Listen to Your Heart

A day in the life of a caregiver is filled with hundreds of decisions. Caregiving requires mental gymnastics—thoughts whirling around in your head keep you in constant problem-solving mode. You do this to survive your days, but the mental and spiritual toll can be harmful.

There are times caregivers should get out of their minds and listen to their hearts. The constant mental chatter needs to be silenced, and meditation is a great way to do this. Squeeze in a few moments each day to sit quietly and just breathe deeply, watching thoughts go by like cars on the road. Sit quietly away from everyone and close your eyes. If you like, you can pray or speak to a higher power and offer up a simple prayer merely asking for help. Promise to listen to your heart and ask for guidance.

Taking this quiet time to slow down your thinking and be open to feeling is like a mini-vacation. It gives you time to focus on your "gut feelings," which are likely not your gut at all but your heart. By quieting your mind, praying, or being open to guidance, that message from your heart gets louder. Listen to it.

Make Coming Unglued a Good Experience

When things build up and become unmanageable, you can become unglued. You may fall into brain fog, feel completely overwhelmed, or like you are losing your mind. Tears are sometimes part of the equation, and feeling guilty and defeated might be in there too.

Even though this makes you feel bad, remember that it doesn't mean you *are* bad. Caregivers come unglued occasionally—all people do. Becoming unglued can even be a good thing if you treat it as such. No one likes to feel unglued, but this feeling is telling you something. Here is a positive way to look at this uncomfortable feeling:

- **Look for the lesson.** What can you learn from this situation? What led up to you feeling unglued? Did you fail to check in with how you were feeling emotionally and physically? Were you neglecting instead of nurturing yourself? Lesson learned! You can now find a solution and be more aware of what you need to do for yourself so this doesn't happen again.
- **Take a break.** You probably would not have given yourself permission to take a break before you came unglued, so now is the perfect time to do so. Go sit quietly, perhaps eat a snack, have a refreshing drink, and take some deep breaths. Coming unglued is also a wonderful time to reach out to another caregiver to commiserate.

Coming unglued is not only permitted; it can also be motivational! Treat it that way, and it can be a good thing!

Look Back, but Don't Stare

The past brings you context, wisdom, and experience. If you are smart about your past, you know it is best when you are reviewing it, not trying to revise it. What is done is done. If you learned something from it, then that lesson is extremely valuable. Caregivers especially can benefit from these lessons and apply that information to similar situations in the present.

Looking in the rearview mirror can be helpful, but you mustn't stare. You can take what you need and leave the rest. Try practicing these tactics when you feel like you can't let go of the past and you are staring too hard at it.

- **Stop going over past experiences.** It's one thing to review something unfortunate that happened or a mistake you made in your caregiving process, but it is another to go over and over it in your mind trying to change the outcome or telling yourself what you should have done. The caregiver learning curve is big, hard, and always there. You did the best that you could at the time. You now know exactly where you stumbled, and you can avoid that bump in the future. Turn off the chatter in your mind by thinking about the future instead and visualizing something great happening.
- **Be grateful for the experience.** As Maya Angelou says, "Do the best you can until you know better. Then when you know better, do better." How can you improve if you don't learn anything new? Where would you be if you didn't have the past to teach you? If you hadn't learned the stove was hot by touching it, you would be burning yourself constantly. No matter how uncomfortable events of the past might have made you, they gave you insight and knowledge and made you better at what you do and who you are. You become a better caregiver by being willing to try out new techniques and methods.

- **Own it.** Everyone makes mistakes. When you do, accept responsibility and face the music. Even if it hurts, stop making excuses. Own up to what your part was, admit you will try to do better, and be grateful that you have learned a lesson.

It's okay if you are glancing in the rearview mirror to help you navigate your caregiving path. However, you will hit something in front of you if you are staring in that rearview mirror and not paying attention to the road ahead. Let the past be helpful, not distracting, demanding, or demeaning. The past is only there as a reference point, and that's where its value lies. Other than that, it is well past its expiration date and should be thrown out.

Be a Self-Aware Caregiver

Self-awareness is one of the most important bricks in the foundation of empowered caregiving. With self-awareness, you can gain valuable insight into who you are and how you navigate your caregiving journey.

When you focus on yourself, your feelings, and your behaviors, you can begin to understand what makes you tick and where you can improve your abilities to be an open and balanced caregiver. You can identify your strengths and see the areas you can change and improve. Your feelings tell you so much about how others affect you, and if you closely observe those feelings, you can find patterns or triggers from your past that might be affecting your behavior.

The following exercises can help you become more self-aware:

- **Practice mindfulness.** Mindfulness is the ability to be present in the moment and to be aware of what you are doing and feeling emotionally and physically in the here and now. Meditation is a wonderful form of mindfulness and can heighten your self-awareness, but finding the time to sit and meditate may not always be possible. Instead, try practicing mindfulness by bringing your attention to the present moment. Pay close attention to whatever you are doing and notice how you are breathing, how your body feels, and what you are feeling inside. You can do this with any task, such as washing the dishes. For example, you could notice the warm water and how the suds and dishes feel, then check in with your body and thoughts. Practice mindfulness often during your day, especially when something bothers or stresses you. This awareness can help you identify what's going on emotionally and physically, which gives you the information you need to work on or heal what's bothering you.
- **Journal it.** If something triggers you or you are behaving in a manner that doesn't feel right, sneak off for a minute and write about it. Even jotting

down a few sentences about what you are feeling can be immensely helpful and insightful. Writing helps to keep you present and aware.

- **Ask others how they see you.** This is a brave action and not for everyone, but the insight gained can be worth the discomfort. Asking others to tell you how they see you in your caregiving role can be extremely helpful. Only do this if you are comfortable, and only do it with people you trust and who support you. You want positive feedback and suggestions, not judgment.

Being self-aware gives you the power to understand how you are acting and why. It's an excellent way to stop anger, guilt, or fear in their tracks because you are aware of the feelings rising, you understand why they are happening, and you can then process these emotions in a healthy way. Self-awareness is a caregiver's secret weapon.

Be Spontaneous

Caregivers should embrace surprise. Being open to spontaneity is a defense against caregiver burnout. If you don't embrace change and work at going with the flow, your rigidity can make your job so much harder. Remember, you cannot control everything.

Try these little adjustments if you want to be a more spontaneous, less rigid caregiver.

- **The next time you are about to say no, say "Why not?"** What do you have to lose? Maybe your loved one wants to do something that you would normally never allow or think is unnecessary or feel is a waste of time or silly. Take a minute to give in to the silly. Nothing is ever lost by doing so, and it might make everybody a little happier.
- **Start with little things.** You do not have to be spontaneous in big ways at first. Just do one thing a little differently, like switching up the way you shop or cook something, or walk in a different direction. Minor changes can be interesting and break up old habits.
- **See the other side of things.** Take one small belief you hold and see if you can approach that belief differently. See if you can have another point of view. Just trying this can stretch your spontaneous muscle.

Trying out new things can not only be healthy and fulfilling; it can also sweep out the cobwebs in your heart and mind and let some fresh air in!

Choose Happiness over Being Right

You cannot change the personalities of those you care for or those you come in contact with. Everyone has their own unique experiences—the person you care for can be very different from you. Sometimes you don't see eye to eye with the person you care for, and you can butt heads with each other. Neither of you may intend for it to happen, but communication can break down, misunderstandings arise, and, before you know it, you are in the middle of an argument. Your need to win your point may supersede your ability to communicate calmly.

When you feel your anger rising and you are about to get into it with someone, ask yourself this question: "Do I want to be right, or do I want to be happy?"

The answer usually is that you want to be happy. Being right can feel important for a minute, particularly if the evidence supports the fact that you are indeed correct, but that satisfaction is brief and usually comes at the expense of the feelings of others. When you refuse to give in because you want to be right, you are asking for uncomfortable conflict.

Being happy is a much better feeling. Choose to be happy and let go of any need to be right. Caregiving brings enough heartache and discomfort. If you can graciously give in to those you care for or interact with and avoid an argument, you are taking the high road with people who probably need a break anyway. It's more important to get along and not waste precious time.

Accept the Big Feelings Caregiving Triggers

Caregivers can often be surprised by the wave of challenging and painful emotions that caregiving brings up. Ignoring the fact that caregiving is fraught with big emotional triggers makes dealing with these emotions harder than it needs to be. You can't safely manage your emotional state without acknowledging it. Try these helpful processing tactics to work through the emotional roller coaster of caregiving.

- Acknowledge the fact that caregiving brings up big feelings. What are those feelings? What are you feeling right now? Ask yourself what you are thinking and how you feel in your heart and head. Don't be afraid to dig up your feelings and shine a light on them.
- Accept the fact that it is normal to be emotionally charged during caregiving. There is nothing wrong with feeling fear, anger, grief, sadness, or even positive emotions like joy. Stop beating yourself up for feeling sad, crying, or feeling frustrated. You are not weak or a bad caregiver. You are human, and everyone is entitled to being upset.
- Share these feelings. Talk about them with people who are good listeners. Write about your feelings. Get to know them and what is causing them.
- Soothe yourself when you can with self-care actions like rest, healthy food, socialization, community support, and any type of therapy that feels comfortable to you.

Big feelings are side effects of caregiving. Get the help you deserve to process them in a healthy, supportive way.

Give Up the Ghosts

Caregivers who choose to care for family members or people who remind them of family members may carry old baggage. The caregiving journey can be fraught with ghosts from the past that can haunt the current relationship.

Since the loved one cannot be expected to erase or resolve your past relationships, the responsibility falls to you. By practicing the following emotional strategies, you can begin to chase the ghosts away and heal any old wounds that affect your current relationships. This can reconcile and rebuild the relationship with those you care for.

- **Try to forgive.** Forgiveness is a valuable emotional tool. You can begin the healing process by letting go of the past that no longer serves you or your loved one. Let go of old injuries and anger. This person did the best they could at the time. You can still set boundaries from this point on.
- **Be empathetic.** Empathy is a powerful skill that can help you relate to others. Look closely at what makes your loved one tick. If they were strangers, how would you treat them? Do pain, fear, or insecurity make them act out? Try empathizing with them instead of resenting them. Begin by being kinder and more loving.
- **Let go of the past.** That was then and this is now. You are an adult and have developed new coping skills. You have your own personal power and do not need to react like your younger self did.

Seek Professional Help

Caregivers often try to soldier on alone. Many of them are stuck with the noble impression that they can manage everything by themselves. Reality can contradict this notion when caregiver burnout or physical and mental health issues crop up due to the staggering demands of caregiving.

Some of the best lessons caregivers can learn is that they do not have to be alone in their role and that it is healthy and acceptable to seek professional help when it's needed. If you are having a hard time with something, whether it's physical, emotional, or the practical aspects of caring for your loved one, it is recommended that you seek professional help for yourself and those you serve. It's not only acceptable; it's necessary if you want to be a healthy, happy, and effective caregiver. Don't be ashamed. All caregivers require help, and the most stable caregivers are those who are not afraid to reach out to professionals for assistance and support.

Asking other caregivers for recommendations is key, as they may have trusted people they use and like. Doctors, social workers, community leaders, and religious organizations may also have suggestions or be able to refer you to someone who can help.

You are entitled to getting all the help you need. Carve out the time to investigate resources, and do not give up until you have found the right professionals to give you the support you need.

Escape Emotional Traps

We all have emotional triggers. Everyone is sensitive about something, and even caregivers can overreact when their buttons are pushed. Since a substantial percentage of caregiving is done by family members, this can create a highly charged relationship and a sensitive emotional situation.

Watch out for signs that you are not as calm and balanced as you could be. If you are centered, you can ignore what others say and do. If you don't have enough emotional bandwidth for a particular situation, your buttons will get pushed. This can set you up to be grouchy and upset. To avoid this emotional trap, catch yourself before you say or do something you may regret later.

When you feel like you are losing control of your emotions, stop and focus on yourself and what you are feeling—forget what anyone else is saying or doing. Notice if you need to take a break or do something that brings you joy or makes you laugh or even gets you away from everyone for a few minutes. Instead of pushing yourself harder, ease up and take it slow. How can you be kind to yourself right now?

It's vital that you stay aware of what's going on with yourself. When you sense you are falling into an emotional trap, you need to turn to whatever self-care routine you need to feel calm and balanced again. Of course, it's understandable that you are overwhelmed and tired, but if you stay aware of your emotional well-being you can pull yourself out of a potentially stressful place.

Manage Your Anger

Caregivers are often given a saintly status, but this can make them feel the need to appear perfect and to never experience reasonable feelings like anger. The reality is that no one has more reason to feel anger than caregivers. What they have to witness, put up with, and battle against would make anyone angry.

If you have periods in your caregiving journey when you feel angry, give yourself the permission to feel it. Anger during the caregiving experience is normal, and emotionally healthy caregivers feel it often. Fighting or stuffing down a wave of anger that is justified and normal only intensifies it.

You need to allow yourself to be angry without shame and blame and find ways to process anger that let you release it healthily. Forgive yourself for being angry and trust that it is an indicator of the need to care for yourself.

It is vital that you reach out and talk about your anger with someone you trust who will listen and give you the space to let loose and describe what you are feeling and why. Afterward, take time to compose yourself and do calming, rejuvenating self-care activities such as taking a hot bath or going for a walk. Remember, the storm will pass, and you will be wiser and stronger.

Acknowledge Grief

Grief is something all caregivers are familiar with. Caregivers expect that they will grieve the loss of their loved ones. As devastating as this is, caregivers feel prepared for this type of grief. It's the grief and anticipatory grief caregivers face during their caregiving that are surprising and sometimes confusing.

These feelings of grief and sadness that you experience when you are taking care of someone come from many different places and have many legitimate reasons. Knowing that those you care for may be nearing their end of life causes anticipatory grief that can be profound and grounded in a sense of future loss. Then there is the sense of loss for life as it used to be or how you would like it to be. Your caregiving job has created a temporary detour for your "normal" life, and grieving that lifestyle is understandable.

Acknowledging and understanding the legitimate sadness you feel around these losses and your right to feel them are the first steps in the process of honoring and moving through them to a point where the grief is present but not debilitating.

Write about your grief and sense of loss to help clarify and identify these feelings. Talk to family and other caregivers about it. Engage with your spiritual leader and share about it. Treating yourself with the same kindness and compassion you would shower on someone you love when they are grieving is key to a healthy grief process for yourself. Be open to it.

Face Your Fear

The fears of caregiving are real and often legitimate. Being responsible for the well-being of someone else carries a heavy burden with it. The future and the unknown loom over you, and it can feel as though at any minute the rug might be pulled out from under you and those you care for.

As a caregiver, fear might feel like a constant companion, but you can practice numerous self-care activities to reduce the effect fear has on you. Work to stay balanced and calm so fear has a harder time digging in and throwing you off balance.

By taking measures to stay calm and relaxed during your caregiving day, you build up resistance to fear. Whether it's meditation, sitting in church, breathing exercises, running, or walking around the block, apply your favorite self-care centering ritual or practice. Fear plays on your mind if you sit there and let it. Fight back by doing something that puts you in your happy place and gives you the strength and reason to feel hopeful and safe.

If you are afraid of a new caregiving duty or task, take small steps toward reaching your goal. Tiny steps add up, and the more time you give yourself to get used to something, the less scary it becomes. If you are afraid of a new situation, go into it slowly. As you get used to it, it will become less scary.

Make sure you focus on the present so you don't get lost in thoughts about the future. It is useless and dangerous to make up scary possibilities of things that might happen. You have no idea what might happen. Tell yourself not to be afraid of anything that isn't real, true, or hasn't happened yet.

Talk to someone else about the fears you are feeling. Other caregivers will certainly understand and relate immediately, and when you share your fear out loud, it shines a light on it. Fear grows in the dark. By getting fear out of your head and heart and out into the open, you stop it from growing. Getting feedback from those who have experienced the same situation you are will give you a new perspective. It reinforces the fact that you are not alone and don't have to face anything by yourself. There's always safety in numbers.

Caregiving is scary. Facing fear is about learning how to live with it. Courage isn't about getting rid of your fear; it's about moving forward in spite of it. When you tackle your fear with reason; physical, emotional, and spiritual balance; serenity; and the support of others who love and believe in you, you can find the strength to work through it. Fear will no longer incapacitate you or cause you to freeze or procrastinate. You can be afraid but not stuck. You can muster up the strength you need to face your fears, and the more you face fear and survive doing so, the faster you conquer it.

Deal With the Caregiver Blues

Caregivers get the blues. Anyone who faces the challenges of caring for someone knows that the biggest challenge is staying positive and hopeful even when the physical and emotional toll that comes with the role can leave you feeling grief and sadness.

For some reason, caregivers often worry and feel guilty about having these feelings of sadness. It's helpful to accept the truth that caregiving is hard and sometimes sad and that these reactions are normal. This allows you to work through the sadness and process it in a healthy way.

When caregiving has you feeling sadness or grief, you can tell yourself it's okay to feel sad. It's normal, understandable, and appropriate. Being patient and gentle with yourself when you get the blues helps to soothe them.

Like most big feelings, the blues need to be acknowledged and processed, not stuffed or ignored. The blues deserve attention and to be honored. There is always a reason for them, and being compassionate about having them is a big step toward sitting with them so they can be experienced and managed.

So don't fight or stuff the caregiver blues. You have them for a reason. Instead of fighting them, share them. Reach out to someone you trust who supports you and be honest about how you are feeling. It's always great if they are caregivers too because they can share their experience, strength, and hope and may have suggestions for what helped them work through the blues.

It's a great idea to join a caregivers' support group so you can get support and help from other caregivers and the group counselor. Ask your doctor, your local Agency on Aging, or the Alzheimer's Association (www.alz.org) if they know of any local caregivers' groups to join or counselors that specialize in supporting caregivers. If your loved one is assigned a social worker, do not hesitate to ask them for recommendations or suggestions for a therapist or group you can contact.

It's always important to discuss with professionals or doctors any overwhelming feelings that are too big to handle alone. If you are feeling depressed to the point where you are stuck and unable to function, reaching out to someone who can help is the right thing to do.

Protect and love yourself during these occasional bouts of the caregiver blues. You are entitled to the same care and attention that those you care for receive for their emotional needs. Getting the blues simply means you are a caring and sensitive person, which is what makes you so successful as a caregiver. Be as kind and loving to yourself as you would be to others and make sure you allow yourself to get the help, support, and encouragement you need and deserve.

Manage Your Worry

It's so natural for caregivers to worry—there are so many scary things that are either going wrong or could go wrong. Every step, every decision, every activity surrounding the well-being of those you care for carries a heavy weight of responsibility with it. Even the little things can be worrisome. Even though caregiving can never be completely worry-free, managing the things you worry about is possible.

Here are a few tricks to help you cope with caregiver worry.

- **Remember that often the things you worry about never happen.** Other things might occur, but the chance that your worries might actually happen is very slim. Think back. Did that thing you were so worried about last week happen?
- **Go over your survival rates.** As you look back on your caregiving experience, were you able to survive most challenges successfully? Highlight your victories, big and small, and remember you are a survivor. You are serving those you care for. Trust that things happen for a reason and in the right way.
- **Write down all your worries.** Like magic, worries look less scary on paper. Plan steps you can take to eliminate the worries on your list and take them!
- **Always remember to share your worries with someone else.** They can offer comfort and might have suggestions to help you take actions that can wipe the worry out.

Forgive yourself for worrying, but don't let it ruin your days.

Understand That It's Okay to Not Be Okay

There are going to be times that caregivers feel bad, off-balance, and upset. This is an understandable reaction to having to be "on" all the time in a challenging situation. You won't always feel your best, and you might begin to feel down, or sad, or exhausted.

The best way to handle this is to know that it's okay to not be okay. You are human, and caregiving is hard. It's okay to have an off day or off week! There's no shame, you are not alone, and you are entitled and allowed. No one expects you to be happy all the time.

Give yourself space. Call your team, let them know what's going on, and see if they can pitch in and give you some time off, even if it's for an afternoon. Take advantage of this time away and spend it with someone who understands what you are going through and makes you feel accepted unconditionally. You need to be around people who make you smile and support you while you rest and relax.

Most importantly, be kind and compassionate to yourself. It happens to the best of us. Sit with it, be consoled, and take the needed time to repair and recharge.

Avoid Perfectionism

A very common issue that most caregivers struggle with is trying to be a perfect caregiver. Admittedly, the stakes are higher in the caregiving role than many other jobs since someone else's health and well-being are on the line, but feeling the need to do everything perfectly causes enormous pressure and sets unrealistic expectations.

Trying to be a perfect caregiver is not only impossible; it can prevent you from taking action because you are so afraid to fail that you freeze. Procrastination is a nasty side effect of perfectionism and can be a nightmare in a caregiver's world.

To avoid perfectionism crippling you, here are some suggestions:

- Begin by remembering that you are human, and all people make mistakes. If it weren't for mistakes, you would never learn anything. Being human and learning from your mistakes makes you a better caregiver.
- Stop trying so hard. The only approval you need is your own. If you are showing up and doing the best you can, nothing can beat that.
- Try being open to experimenting with things rather than doing them perfectly. Be curious instead of cautious. Just try things instead of worrying about justifying how you do them.
- Ask your loved ones how well you are doing your job and if they feel loved and supported by you. They will have the perfect answer.

Get Rid of the Guilt

When asked, most caregivers say they feel guilty about a variety of things. Some say they feel guilty that they don't do enough for those they serve, and most say they feel guilty if they take time away from their caregiving to care for themselves. This guilt prevents caregivers from taking the self-care actions that ironically make them better caregivers.

Stop putting unrealistic expectations on yourself as a caregiver. You don't have to be perfect; you just have to show up. There is no rule book and no end goal to achieve other than supporting those you care for. You do that by being understanding and loving. The mere fact that you are available to make their lives better is the only accomplishment you need to be concerned with.

If you must feel guilty when it comes to your self-care, feel guilty that you don't do it enough. Self-care doesn't benefit just you; when you take care of yourself, you are stronger, more patient and compassionate, and have more energy for the job. Self-care makes you the best caregiver you can be.

As an exercise, the next time you feel guilty about taking some "me time," take it anyway. Do this every time you feel guilty about self-care. Pretty soon the positive results will outweigh the guilty feelings, and before you know it, you will be happier and free of guilt.

Trust Yourself

One of the side effects of caregiving is self-doubt. Caregivers may sometimes worry whether or not they have what it takes to be a great caregiver.

The secret to facing these doubts and concerns is learning to trust yourself. You have chosen caregiving as your purpose and even when things are unfamiliar or new, you have the power to do your best. You don't have to do it perfectly and you don't have to know all the answers. If you follow your heart, you can't go wrong.

Leaning on the things you do well, the memories of your successes, and your ability to survive demanding situations in the past are helpful self-trust–building tools. Everything you've learned in your life so far has prepared you to be an amazing caregiver. Recall and write those memories down and review them often. They are solid reminders and proof you are reliable and capable.

Write down your concerns and be willing to honestly share them with people who honor and appreciate you. Ask them to describe the qualities they see in you that they value. Let them tell you why they trust and depend on you.

Build up your self-trust with self-care, don't be afraid to be vulnerable and open, be kind and forgiving to yourself if you have an occasional stumble, and listen to that voice inside that says you are unique and special. Trust yourself, your heart, and the love you have for those you care for. This will guide you through any situation.

Chapter 2: Self-Care for Your Body

The physical requirements of caregiving are intense. Caregiving is a marathon, not a sprint, and the best way to survive the demands made by caregiving on your body is to be prepared. Neglecting your body is not an option. You must take every opportunity to maintain or improve your health and stay in the best physical shape as you run your caregiving marathon.

This chapter discusses the daily choices you should make to remain healthy and strong and offers easy-to-manage activities you can do to ensure you are a fit caregiver. These include physical exercise and movement as well as nurturing and relaxing actions that treat and replenish the whole body and its relationship to your mind and spirit. A good combination of movement, awareness, pampering, and positive and pleasant sensory techniques creates a strong whole-body experience.

Since each caregiving situation is unique and time allowances vary from caregiver to caregiver, there are numerous activities offered in this chapter that can be done in any amount of time, anywhere, on any schedule. The secret is in the doing. All the tools you need to maintain consistent physical wellness and the energy you need to fulfill your role are included here for easy access. The stronger and healthier you feel, the easier you can adapt to the rigors of caregiving.

Pace Yourself

If you were running a marathon, you wouldn't shoot out of the gate at full speed, trying to keep that pace the entire race. You would set a good solid gait to preserve your precious energy so you could finish the race. It's not about how fast; it's about being steady.

Caregiving is like running a marathon. You need to pace yourself and save your energy for the long haul. You may want to take care of everyone and everything immediately, but that's just not possible.

You need to set a realistic pace and attainable goals. Slow down and focus on the task at hand and the things right in front of you. Take a good, hard look at what your priorities are and pick three that are the most important. Then decide what actions you need to take to get those priorities met, and create a plan to tackle them in a time frame that feels doable and comfortable. It might be good to run this action plan by someone else for feedback and a fresh perspective. Remember to delegate tasks and actions to others whenever possible, and if you begin to feel overwhelmed, take a break immediately. Once you are refreshed and recharged, start back up slow and steady, keeping an even pace with one foot in front of the other, and maintaining your priorities. Everything you need to get done will get done, and the rest can wait until tomorrow.

Think of Yourself As an Athlete

Caregivers need to think of themselves as athletes. To avoid caregiver burnout, you must be fit, strong, resilient, and disciplined. When you see successful athletes, you know that discipline, training, and respect for their body and mind got them to where they are and contribute to their success. That same respect that athletes have for their bodies and minds can be applied to how you treat yourself during your caregiving journey.

You can begin to build this dedication by embracing the idea that your job as a caregiver requires Herculean physical and emotional strength, and you must do everything you can to build up your body, mind, and spirit, beginning with keeping your body in the best possible shape.

This means making sure that, before all else, you are making staying fit a priority. To ensure this becomes and stays a priority, you must pledge to respect and care for yourself as any other athlete would. Eat the right foods, schedule exercise and training into your day, get help from others to keep you on track, and take the needed rest and downtime required to always be at your best.

Prioritizing your health like this is not easy when caregiving, but no one has ever won a gold medal because it was easy. By adopting the mindset of an athlete and prioritizing yourself, you set yourself up to win.

Eat Like a Champion

Caregivers are champions for those they care for. The best way to be a champion and meet that challenge is to be in tip-top shape. One of the most important components of being in shape is eating healthy food. What and how you eat matters enormously, because how you maintain your physical well-being and strength depends on how you fuel your body.

Every athletic champion in the world has a healthy diet as the cornerstone of their program and routine to ensure their success and enhance their performance. Studies prove that a healthy body and mind require proper nutrition and hydration, and the strongest and highest-performing people consider healthy eating essential to maintaining the optimal physical and mental state to experience peak performance.

You need to eat fresh, healthy, nutritious meals consistently. This self-care routine is essential to being able to withstand the storms of caregiving and avoiding caregiver burnout.

It's true that it's not always easy to plan meals or stay on schedule to eat them, but the same energy it takes to buy potato chips, fast food, processed foods, and soda can be spent ensuring that vegetables, healthy snacks, and protein are in the shopping cart and refrigerator for everyone in the caregiving circle. It's so much easier to reach for healthy snacks and healthy meal choices if they are waiting in the kitchen.

Junk food can be a comfort food, and it's hard to find time to cook, sit, and relax while eating when you are a caregiver. However, you can choose food that offers you greater benefits in the long run and do your best to make sure you eat those foods regularly. You make sure those you care for eat well; you should spend the same time and energy on meeting your own needs.

Make the right choices when you shop by getting everyone fruit, vegetables, whole grains, protein, and snacks that are low in sugar and high in nutritional value. Forget the processed foods. Treats are always permitted in moderation, and they should make up the smallest percentage of the cart. No one is saying you have to take away your loved one's favorite cookies; just try substituting fruit occasionally or another healthy snack. Comfort food has a place, but keep it to a minimum.

When you cook for and feed those you care for, make the meals as healthy as possible and make enough for you. Do a healthy version of their meal for yourself if need be. Then sit everyone down to dinner and eat with them if possible. You have your loved ones eating on a schedule that's like clockwork; make it work for you too, so you all get nourishment and companionship. Then you will all be eating like champions.

Dance

There's something about letting loose on a dance floor or even in the living room that makes everyone smile. Everybody knows what it's like to just get up and dance and experience the joy of moving around to music without a care in the world.

When you are knee-deep in medications and bandages and caring for someone in pain and discomfort, probably the last thing you can imagine doing is dancing. But this is exactly when you need to make sure you go out of your way to practice self-care activities. You need to enjoy the pleasures of life and participate in activities that take you away from the stress and challenges you are facing.

Dancing in the kitchen or any room in the house that suits you is one of those activities. All it takes is a minute to put on a song and let it all go! If those you care for are able, they can join in. Playing something they listened to in their youth is always a hit. Even if in a wheelchair or bedridden, they can swing their arms, wave their hands, or nod their heads and join in. You may be surprised at the reaction you get from them. The stimulation may be just what they need, and you can both have fun together!

Dress for Success

There is nothing wrong with sweatpants, yoga outfits, slippers, and comfy T-shirts. Being comfortable is soothing and makes it easy to handle spills, vacuum, clean the bathroom, and help bathe your loved one. Unless you are at the doctor's office, in the emergency room, taking those you care for out for a stroll, or grocery shopping, who sees you? Why bother dressing up?

Occasionally, you may want to spruce things up a bit because while others might not see you, you see you. By making a special effort to pick out a nice outfit that makes you feel good about yourself, you can get an endorphin boost and put yourself in a good mood. Dressing up and looking your best boosts your self-worth and can make you feel empowered to take on the day.

Shop in your closet and try new combinations or wear favorite outfits. If your mornings typically begin in a "hit the ground running" kind of way, pick out a fun outfit the night before. That effort alone signals your brain that tomorrow is special and something to look forward to. Dressing up affects the way you feel, act, and think and can even help you face the day with a more positive attitude.

If chucking the sweatpants feels like too much of a hassle, schedule a dress-up day once a week. Maybe instead of casual Friday, have a look-like-a-million-bucks Friday. Once you start to feel the difference you might dress up all week!

Hydrate

One of the first things you were probably taught or learned when you became a caregiver is that you must keep those you care for hydrated, especially if they are elderly. The sense of being thirsty declines with age, so the elderly lose their desire to drink water and can become dehydrated. Dehydration is one of the leading causes of hospitalization in the elderly. It can cause organ failure and major complications.

So here you are, hovering over your loved one doing everything you can to keep them hydrated (preferably with water) and yet you forget to keep hydrated yourself! Once again, you are paying attention to the needs of those you serve and ignoring those needs in yourself. Staying hydrated is critical to being a balanced, healthy caregiver.

Water plays an important part in almost every function of the body. It lubricates your joints and balances your temperature; is responsible not only for digestion but also helping get rid of both solid and liquid waste; makes up 60 percent of your body; keeps your organs (especially the kidneys), skin, and blood pressure healthy. Not to mention, if you don't drink enough water to replace what your body uses up, your thinking and reasoning can be negatively affected.

You need to hydrate right along with those you care for. Studies say that men should drink approximately 3.7 liters and women 2.7 liters a day. Most sources recommend drinking eight glasses of water a day, which is about equal to a 2-liter bottle of water.

This may sound like an impossible job with everything else you must do. However, caregivers are prone to forget to drink. That means you must pay attention to how much water you are drinking during your day and be proactive even when you are not thirsty.

Kick it off as soon as you get up in the morning by drinking a glass of water before your coffee, tea, or juice. You dehydrate during the night, and by drinking water first thing you are replenishing what you lost. Then, as you go through your day helping your loved ones stay hydrated, participate yourself and hydrate along with them. Add another glass especially before or after that glass of wine before bed!

To keep everyone on the hydration track, you can set a timer on your phone to remind yourself to grab a glass or bottle and sip it with your loved one. It can become a fun break time. Keeping track of everyone's fluid intake is yet another way to maintain everyone's health. Hydrate, and your body will smile!

Don't Skip Meals—Snack

Although they don't mean to, caregivers sometimes skip meals. Often at the end of the day or even halfway through it, you will look up from something you are doing, wondering what time it is, and realize you haven't eaten all day. You need to refuel just like a car, or you run out of gas. And that can be bad not only for you but for your loved ones as well.

No caregiver wants to run out of fuel, and you can always use the added strength and energy food gives you. You don't want to get so caught up in taking care of others that you neglect your own needs, including the need for regular, healthy meals.

So, just as you do for your loved ones, you can try to schedule your eating times and plan healthy meals, but when all else fails, try adding in healthy snack times. This works great for them, and you should also take advantage of the tactic!

Find a bunch of healthy protein bars and snacks you like and keep them handy so you see them often and can grab them easily. Set a timer for every few hours, and when it goes off grab a bar or snack. Try to take five minutes to savor it. You need to pump yourself up with the proper nourishment to keep the caregiving train chugging along.

Keep Up with Your Grooming

Making sure those you care for are keeping up with their grooming is something every caregiver will have to deal with. As those you care for get older or feeble or begin to decline physically or mentally, bathing and showering can become difficult, and they begin to resist this activity.

Caregivers understand how important it is and how wonderful it can feel to be showered, bathed, comfy, and groomed and may have to invent creative strategies and tactics to convince their loved ones of this same fact. Transfer this inventive determination into a self-care grooming routine time for you! You deserve the same pampered treatment. Feeling refreshed and clean, with hair washed and styled and nails trimmed, gives you a completely new lease on life. Hitting that restart button is much easier when you look and smell great!

Reach out to family and friends and ask them to take over the caregiving duties for an afternoon so you can get a manicure, pedicure, or haircut, or they can spot you for an hour or so while you take a long, hot shower or a relaxing, luxurious bath with all the trimmings. Carve out this time to keep up with all the things you used to do to make yourself look like a million bucks. Just because you care for others and their grooming habits doesn't mean you can neglect yours. Taking the time to pamper yourself immediately makes your life feel more manageable.

Use *YouTube* As Your Personal Trainer

Can you imagine being a caregiver thirty years ago with no Internet, no social media, and no smartphones? Granted, social media most certainly has its downside, but the wealth of information that's available at your fingertips is astonishing and powerful!

YouTube is a great site for videos of all kinds and can bring a lifetime of educational tools and information to you. Caregivers can watch any type of exercise program they want and can view it at any time of the day and night for free! Hundreds of thousands of videos are available for any subject imaginable, especially for physical health, well-being, and exercise.

Set aside fifteen to twenty minutes in your day, then download *YouTube* from your app store if you don't already have it on your phone, tablet, or TV. Search for the type of exercise you consider fun or at least doable.

Be specific about how much time you can realistically spend on a workout and add that to your search. For instance, type in "8-minute abs," "10-minute cardio," "20-minute complete workout," and voilà! You will find numerous workouts to choose from and some great personal trainers you can return to day after day. Remember also to start slow and easy and seek approval from your primary care doctor for the type of workout you are interested in.

Cardio and full-body workouts are just the tip of the iceberg. There are terrific yoga, tai chi, Zumba, dance, and martial art workouts as well. Some of the best personal trainers in the world are on *YouTube*. Search around and hook up with one as part of your daily self-care time.

Finding the necessary "me time" for this activity may seem hard in the beginning. Choosing easy, short videos to watch makes developing the habit less of a chore. An eight-minute stretching video may be all you can handle in the beginning, and that is fine. As you progress, try to investigate longer videos and find more time for yourself to do them. If you skip a day or two, you can always go back to it and check it out again. That's the beauty of this type of personal trainer. They don't know when you are watching, and there's no judgment!

Make Doctors' Appointments for Yourself

How quickly did you call the doctor recently when your loved one developed a new symptom, had a change in their health, or complained about a new pain? It's probably safe to say that you jumped up and were on the phone immediately, calling their doctor to make an appointment to see them.

Now let's talk about how closely you monitor the time between the wellness or annual physical appointments for those under your care. If you are like most caregivers, you make sure you are on top of scheduling wellness appointments, and when it comes to going to that appointment, you are prepared. Making sure your loved ones have regular checkups is an excellent way to keep track of their health and avoid surprises down the road.

It is extremely important to pay the same attention to your own health and well-being. Why should it be any different for you if something doesn't feel right or you experience pain or discomfort? You need to ring the same alarm bell and address your symptoms just as quickly as you address those of your loved ones. You also need to have regular physicals to avoid those same surprises you dread experiencing with your loved ones. Quite simply, who will take care of them if you get sick?

Start right now and consider how you are feeling and if anything needs to be checked. Is there something that's been bothering you that you keep putting off because you don't have the time? Have you had a checkup recently? Have you sat down with your primary care doctor to discuss your caregiving responsibilities and the stress you are under? Seeking your doctor's advice about stress relief, diet, exercise, and overall health can make a difference in how you approach your lifestyle. Keeping your doctor in the loop and getting anything that concerns or has been bothering you looked at and treated just makes good sense. Getting treatment for something when it's minor and easy to fix sure beats waiting until it's something more serious.

Make an appointment today with your primary care doctor or any other specialist you need to see. If you are lucky enough to be able to pull it off, have the nurse schedule you right after or before a visit for your loved one. You will be surprised at how accommodating the office will be when you explain what's going on. Invest in your health so you can be strong and healthy for those who need you.

Manage Fatigue and Sleep Deprivation

Did you have another sleepless night? Or are you exhausted and nodding in your cereal in the morning or your supper at night? Sleep deprivation and fatigue are common caregiver side effects. While there's no quick cure other than getting as much sleep as possible as soon as you can to catch up, there are some handy tricks to making fatigue a little less unpleasant.

- **First, eat something that is good for you.** Make something yummy and healthy. Something that will refuel you and give you the energy to keep going: protein, balanced carbs, fruit, and vegetables. If you don't feel hungry, make a healthy drink or eat a protein bar. Don't fast, fuel!
- **Second, stop worrying about how bad the day will be or how tired you are.** Just show up, go slow, and do one thing at a time.
- **Next, lower your expectations and just do the minimum.** Today might not be the day you conquer Mount Everest. That's okay. You don't have to climb the mountain every day. You just have to hang out in the camp and give it another try tomorrow. Just make sure everyone is safe and sound, including yourself, and do the best you can. That is good enough.

The best way to cope with fatigue is to go with it. Fuel your body, take it easy, and stop pushing. Tomorrow's a new day.

Go to the Bathroom

Is it really necessary to add this to our activities and actions for self-care? It is! This is less about your physical needs than it appears. Surely, we will all pay the price if we choose not to go to the bathroom when we should, but for caregivers this oversight becomes a much bigger issue. The fact is, caregivers have been known to lose all sense of commitment to their own needs while concentrating on the needs of those they care for.

This single-minded focus on others takes up some of the focus you need for yourself. Those you care for deserve all the attention you can give them, but you deserve attention too. Taking a bathroom break should not have guilt or worry built into it. You are entitled to a calm, restorative time in the bathroom without feeling as though you have a clock to beat. So make sure you go to the bathroom!

Closing that bathroom door should signal to everyone, including you, that you are now going to take a few minutes to regroup and freshen up. You should approach going to the bathroom as a much-needed break. You should look forward to it, plan it, take advantage of it, and demand it! Use it as a symbol of all the things you are allowed to do for yourself without thinking about it or feeling guilty about it.

Look for Warning Signs of Caregiver Burnout

Caregiver burnout is real and dangerous. It's also sneaky because it builds up slowly and then hits like a hurricane. Most of the time it feels like it comes out of nowhere without warning, but there are ways to catch it before it happens or at least lessen its impact.

The best way to avoid caregiver burnout is to be committed to regular, consistent self-care. Rest, healthy eating, socialization, exercise, self-awareness, respite, and recharging are instrumental in building up a wall of resistance against the tsunami of caregiver burnout. If you get lazy about your self-care, you need to be on the lookout for burnout warning signs, so you can take the appropriate actions to nip the burnout in the bud before it overtakes you.

Take heed immediately if you notice any of the following warning signs:

- **Exhaustion.** Caregiving is strenuous and demanding. There is a deep, almost unbearable exhaustion that can set in. If you can't seem to get enough rest or sleep to feel caught up, and you feel like you can't go on, it's time to get help. Reach out and have someone step in so you can get some serious downtime.
- **Losing your cool.** Having patience slip away to the point where you can't handle anything calmly is a big sign that you need to do something for yourself. Get out, take a break, pick that hobby up, exercise, get a haircut, whatever helps you decompress.
- **Feeling defeated.** It's hard to be positive the entire time you are caring for someone, and feeling discouraged is not unusual. Feeling defeated, however, is a warning sign. Pick up the phone and talk it over with another caregiver or trusted, loving ally.
- **Physical pains.** Headaches, backaches, stomachaches, and sleeplessness are some of the many physical signals that you need to slow down, rest, and regroup. Instead of popping an Advil, get a physical, in addition to taking a

break or getting a massage. Pay attention to these symptoms and address them right away.

- **Frequent mood shifts.** If there is a big shift in your moods, from irritation to anger or worry, this is also cause for concern. Now is the time to pause, breathe, meditate, and take stock. Look at the rest you are getting, the way you are eating, the time you are taking for yourself, and make adjustments that fortify your self-care immediately.

Caregiving brings with it a wide range of emotional reactions. Adjusting to and managing this vast range takes great strength. Sometimes it may feel like you are out of control, and this may be because you are on the brink of burnout. This is the time to remember you are not alone. Seek professional help or spiritual guidance if you feel the need, and always share your feelings with people you trust on a regular basis. Avoid letting emotions build up, but if they become overwhelming, sound the alarm to those who support you. Heeding the warning signs of caregiver burnout is the ultimate self-care for caregivers.

Pay Attention to Your Headache

Caregiving brings all sorts of headaches, some metaphorical and some physical. It's the physical ones that help you to hear your body's message to you. A physical headache sends a very strong, clear message that something is wrong and needs to be addressed and changed right away.

Should you experience headaches often or if something feels off, go to the doctor and have an exam. Seeing a doctor to eliminate the possibility of an issue that needs attention is always the best idea. If nothing serious is going on, the doctor has at least been alerted to your condition, and they will probably advise you to calm down and take better care of yourself. This is exactly what most caregivers need to be reminded of. Having a doctor remind you of it might drive it home.

The next time you get a simple stress headache, give it a warm reception. Take it as a sign that you have probably been neglecting yourself in the service of others, and your headache is the product of that neglect. Don't beat yourself up about this neglect, but do listen to the pounding in your temples and admit that it could have been avoided with some nurturing and self-care. Self-care is not something you do after you have fulfilled all your caregiving; it's something you need to do **while** you are caregiving.

Train Your Brain

Physical exercise is a practical self-care tactic all caregivers must have in their self-care toolbox. Exercise for the brain is just as important and should be in that caregiver's self-care toolbox as well. Focus, stamina, memory, and cognitive function are all important ingredients in the healthy caregiver recipe.

You don't have to sit and do puzzles all day; you can train and stimulate your brain by simply trying something new and challenging. Your brain loves to learn new things. Learning a new language or how to play an instrument, quilting, card games, painting, and even teaching some of these skills to others all train your brain. Bumping up your vocabulary, trying new apps, or learning new software are all ways to fire up your brain function.

While there is never enough downtime in the caregiving world, there is plenty of "waiting" time. Sitting at a bedside or in waiting rooms offers the opportunity to practice a new skill. Our loved ones might even be able to join in if the new skill is something that can be done with someone else.

As with any new skill or hobby, practice makes perfect, and training your brain works best when you are consistently working on it. So that means that even if you are not good at the new skill right off the bat, the more you do it, the smarter your brain gets!

Get Out in Nature

Self-care does not have to be complicated. Caregivers should be prioritizing their own well-being in every phase of their caregiving journey, not just on special occasions or when it's almost too late. Everyday activities or actions should be implemented to keep you humming along.

One very simple activity is to make time to get out of your caregiving situation and into nature. This doesn't necessarily have to be a camping trip; it can be a fifteen-minute break. As long as there is fresh air, trees, and reasonable quiet, you are good to go. A local park with walkways or trails and a bench or two or even the backyard are perfect for this activity.

Get out and take a walk around a park. If there's a pond, feed the ducks. If there's a bench, stop and sit quietly, paying attention to the sounds and movements around you. Breathe in deeply and smell the flowers, trees, leaves, or cut grass. Hold your face up to the breeze and let it float over you. Listen to the birds, crickets, squirrels, and children playing.

If you are lucky enough to be able to get away to hike or spend quality time in a preserve or national park, that's even better. But even a quick break to walk and sit under trees to take in the peace and quiet will help restore your body and mind and recharge your caregiver spirit.

Book a Massage

Caregivers experience lots of physical strain during their workday. Caregiving requires strong bodies as well as strong minds. Lots of lifting, shifting, standing, pushing, and pulling are going on. The demands you make on your body not only wear you out; they also make you sore and tense. Just like an athlete, you must keep your body conditioned and recharged. You need to stay flexible and healthy.

Caregivers need to treat those tired muscles with love and respect, and they will always benefit from a relaxing and restorative massage. Scheduling time for a massage is a positive way to treat yourself and your muscles.

Find the time to book a massage. If a full hour seems impossible, find out if your local salon does a ten-minute neck massage. Even ten to fifteen minutes can do the trick to relieve the tension and strain you are carrying around.

If the budget is tight, drop hints about dreaming of a massage to family and friends. Some of them may have been looking to do something for you, and this could be the perfect idea. Also, check to see if there is a massage school nearby. Massage schools offer great massages for half the price.

Don't make excuses, do it! Book a massage! It will put a spring in your step, and your body will thank you the next time you are pushing that wheelchair or lifting your loved one.

Tune In to Your Body

You often hear about caregivers needing to work on self-awareness when it comes to their emotions and mental health. Yet being in tune with your body is just as important. Physical self-awareness is a beautiful thing; it helps you stay in touch with your body and any messages it's sending to you about the state of your health.

Try these awareness activities so you can be aware when your body is trying to tell you something. If you are experiencing pain or discomfort anywhere, make sure you address that right away.

- **Check in with your body as soon as you wake up.** Are you rested and refreshed? If not, take whatever precautions are needed to preserve what energy you have. Hydrate and make sure you eat a good breakfast.
- **Check in with your body during the day.** If you are stiff, get up and stretch. Are you hungry? Take a break and eat! Sit quietly for a few minutes and notice if you are tense or anxious. Take some deep breaths and see if you can visualize a warm, sunny day. Let the tension out.
- **Before going to bed, unplug, switch off, and sit quietly.** Take inventory of how you are feeling and see if you can get your body to wind down by taking deep breaths and paying attention to your breathing. Thank your body for helping you get through your day successfully.

Taking the time to stay in tune with your body is a terrific way to maintain health and happiness.

Avoid Drugs and Excessive Alcohol

No one wants to deny the deserving caregiver a chance to relax and enjoy a glass of beer, wine, or whatever they choose. But it is wise to keep moderation in mind when partaking in alcohol. Using alcohol or recreational drugs to drown out caregiver burnout, pain, or stress can be a serious problem.

Although it is completely understandable that caregivers need to reduce stress, relax, and find an outlet for all the physical and emotional aches and pains, trying to numb them with habits that only make them worse creates a cycle that's damaging and depleting.

You need to limit your alcohol consumption and avoid recreational drugs. It may feel good in the moment to take a hit or have a few extra glasses, but in the long run, you can never be in the top shape you need to be in if you are consuming unhealthy amounts of alcohol or any substance that dehydrates, depresses, or dulls you.

Be honest with yourself if you feel you are leaning on artificial means to get through stress or numb out pain. Talk to someone about it and get help if you need it. That way you can understand what you are doing and learn how to prevent it before it gets worse. There are always alternative ways to unwind and recharge.

Limit Caffeine

There's nothing like a great cup of coffee or tea as soon as you wake up to get you going for your caregiver day. Then there's that cup at lunch and maybe another one midafternoon that hits the spot and recharges you for the rest of your day.

While taking breaks throughout your day is a great self-care activity, ingesting too much caffeine or caffeine later in the day can make you jittery and make it hard to calm down properly at bedtime. You may feel like it's giving you extra energy during the day, but since it takes a while to go through your system, this added caffeine can prevent you from getting the rest you need.

Limit the amount of caffeine you ingest and make sure you also avoid drinking it after lunch. This way it can wear off in time for bed and won't make you jumpy. You don't have to limit your caffeine intake all at once. You should ease up on caffeine slowly, as you might experience slight physical discomfort if you try to quit cold turkey.

Continue to take your lunch and midafternoon breaks since they are the real energizing activities. Just because you aren't drinking coffee, it doesn't mean you won't have lots of other delicious options. There are wonderful decaf coffees and teas (although they might have a small amount of caffeine) and even more amazing caffeine-free herbal options. Sit back and sip without depleting your system.

Invest In the Perfect Shoes

When discussing all the stress and strain on caregivers, the first area everyone seems to focus on is the emotional side. It's easy to see the tension and anxiety caregivers often exhibit. What can be harder to see is the physical toll caregiving can take on caregivers. They put up with aches, pains, and muscle strain, without complaint, but this physical discomfort is just as important to address as the emotional.

By acknowledging the strain caregiving has on your body and pledging to do everything you can to avoid or minimize it, you can limit the damage. One of the best self-care actions you can take is to make sure you are wearing the best shoes to support your physical exertion. Here are some things to look for when shopping for the right shoes that will give you both comfort and practicality.

- Always consider the fit. They should never be too tight or inflexible.
- Look for shoes that offer great posture and arch support.
- They should be slip-resistant.
- They should be easy to take off and easy to clean.
- They should be lightweight but sturdy.

There is an extensive variety of shoes for the nursing and caregiving field, and whether they are sneakers or clogs, they are usually great at supporting your back, your long hours, and the general running around you do as you care for others. Invest in good shoes that work with you.

Take Your Vitamins

Vitamins are not only good for those you care for; they are good for you as well. Caregivers tend to forget to take their vitamins even when they are nagging their loved ones to take theirs! Make sure you maintain a healthy habit of taking any vitamins or supplements that are right for you. This can include a multivitamin and any additional vitamins you might need.

If you are unsure about the many vitamin and supplement products on the market today, you should ask your primary care doctor. Since you have promised yourself that annual checkups are part of your caregiver self-care, you have the perfect opportunity to seek advice and get set up with a vitamin routine during this visit. Annual blood work is usually suggested, and this will provide your doctor with all the information they need to suggest the perfect vitamin regimen for you. Always make sure you remind the doctor that you are a caregiver, so they understand the physical demands you face and the stress you are under.

Making sure you take your vitamins sends a strong message to your body and mind that your health is important to you and you care about it. When you neglect daily self-love habits like taking vitamins, the message is that you don't matter. You do matter! Especially to those you care for and serve, so send the proper message!

Do Cardio!

Caregivers have big hearts, so it's extremely important to keep them healthy and pumping out all that love. Doing cardio exercise is the perfect way to keep your heart and body in tip-top shape. Cardio or aerobic exercise is anything that increases your heart and breathing rate for a minimum of ten minutes. Cardio strengthens your heart and sends more oxygen to your brain and muscles. This sends lots of love to your entire body, builds up your immune system, helps you sleep, and releases endorphin hormones, which are believed to relieve stress and anxiety.

Examples of cardio exercise are running, dancing, biking, and swimming. But raking leaves, power walking the hallway, or jumping jacks in the living room can also fit the bill. It's recommended that caregivers do thirty to sixty minutes of cardio four to six times a week.

Don't worry if you can't find a full thirty minutes to do cardio. You can break it up into two fifteen-minute sessions a day, and do it four days a week if that's what you can manage. When you begin to add cardio into your day, take it slow and build up your tolerance.

Remember, if something like running or swimming seems out of reach, dancing is also considered a great cardio workout. All you have to do is put on your favorite music for fifteen minutes twice a day and dance like nobody's watching.

Indulge In Facials

When was the last time you had a facial? Making time to pamper that gorgeous face of yours that works so hard to keep a smile going all day long for those you care for is a must!

This activity can even be shared with your loved one if they would like to participate and are able to enjoy it. You can both be pampered while your normal caregiving routine and face get a refreshing boost!

Your local pharmacy, grocery, and big-box stores have a variety of inexpensive one-application facials. Opt for a gentle facial for sensitive skin and check that the ingredients are safe for your loved one. There are also great do-it-yourself powder facial products that you can mix with water or apple cider vinegar.

If you prefer a fun, do-it-yourself gentle mixture from your kitchen, you can blend equal parts crushed oats and plain Greek yogurt with a dash of honey into a paste for your face and top it off with two cucumber slices for your eyes! Rinse with warm water after ten to fifteen minutes. There are wonderful homemade facial recipes like these to be found online!

Taking the time to nurture and pamper yourself with a facial is not only good for your skin and body; it's good for your soul and keeps away the caregiver blues. If you can share this experience with someone you care for, even better! You will both glow!

Pamper Your Gut

When you have a healthy gut, all is right with the world. Your food is broken down into healthy, rich, fuel and nutrients that give you energy, support your brain function, and keep your immune system humming and fighting off infection.

To maintain the healthiest gut possible, you need to pay attention to what you put in it. This isn't about diets that help you gain or lose weight or overdoing or correcting food consumption; it's about eating foods that support you and your gut health.

The goal is to eat a combination of whole grains, proteins, fruits, and vegetables. Things to avoid are soda or sugary drinks and lots of caffeine or alcohol and sweets. You could also see a nutritionist who can make a personalized eating plan just for you.

In addition to making good food choices, getting plenty of rest, lowering your stress levels, and drinking lots of water will keep your tummy healthy and happy. Also try to make sure only good gut-healthy foods are in your refrigerator and limit the amount of sweets in the house.

When you are serious about having a healthy gut, you are being serious about your entire well-being. Make your whole body happy by keeping your gut healthy.

Practice Yoga

The word "yoga" is based on the Sanskrit word for "yoke," "unity," or "union," and it describes making a connection between the mind and body and spirit of the universe. It's a wonderful physical practice perfect for caregivers.

One of the benefits of yoga is that you practice breathing exercises along with physical movement and have the chance to clear and still your mind. So you are not only getting the physical workout; you are also performing deep breathing along with receiving guided instructions to help you calm your mind.

Finding a yoga class that is perfect for you and figuring out how much time you can spare and when you can spare it is extremely easy. There are so many terrific classes of various lengths and levels (from beginners to advanced) and great professional teachers to be found online. You don't have to leave the house, and many of the lessons are free! There is even chair yoga that you might do with those you care for.

Start with beginners' classes and take it slow. Build up to more advanced classes, but remember to never strain yourself. Yoga is about being where you are, not where you think you should be. Once you get hooked on a class, teacher, or style, you can add it to your schedule. Yoga can be there for you as a wonderful escape and balancing self-care activity.

Hire Someone to Help

There might come a time in your caregiving when you just can't do all the lifting yourself, physically or figuratively. It's difficult doing it alone. This might be the time to get over all the reservations you have about adding a new person to the mix and consider hiring someone.

Depending on budget and actual need, there are several options, including using an agency to help you hire an aide or certified professional caregiver. This can be a complicated process, and it may take a while to get the perfect person to give you the backup you need. Keeping this process organized and being clear about what you need and want can greatly reduce the stress around it.

Write down the issues you are struggling with and the exact tasks you are willing to delegate. Be honest with yourself and be as realistic as possible. Let go of things that are too much for you to handle.

Make a list of tasks in each category of issues. Calculate the time in hours it takes you to accomplish each task and write the hours next to the task. When you are finished, list the tasks and hours associated with them in order of importance, with the ones you desperately need help with at the top of the list.

Now you have a clear, organized list of tasks and the hours they require to get the help you need. Depending on the budget, you can get as much relief as you can afford with the most pressing needs.

Breathe for Balance

People often take breathing for granted. You may think that since your body automatically takes care of your breathing you can ignore it. In actuality, during your caregiving experience, you might be taking shallow, rapid breaths when you are anxious or stressed without even noticing it, and this can add to your stress, making your body tense and lowering your energy.

Being aware of how you are breathing, and taking the time to practice some deep breathing, is a surprisingly easy but extremely effective way to feel better. It can help lower your heart rate, build up your immunity, and lower your blood pressure.

Try these breathing exercises to calm down, reset your body, and soothe your caregiver soul.

Belly Breathing

- Sit or lie in a comfortable position.
- Place one hand on your belly and the other hand on your chest.
- Breathe in deeply for a count of 3.
- The hand on your chest should remain still, while the hand on your belly should move up and down because, as you breathe, your belly (or diaphragm) is expanding like a balloon.
- Breathe out for a count of 3 and push in your belly so it collapses as the air goes out.
- Do this as often as possible for five to eight minutes each day.

This technique reminds you to take the time to breathe in deeply and fully and sends a message to your brain and body to chill out. It's a perfect little self-care break during a hectic day in the life of a caregiver.

The next breathing exercise, 4-7-8 breathing, is great for stress reduction especially before sleep, as it may help relax your body so you can get the rest you need. It's a breathing pattern based on pranayama, or yoga breathing, and the technique was developed by Dr. Andrew Weil.

4-7-8 Breathing

- Sit or lie down in a comfortable position.
- Breathe in through your nose for a count of 4.
- Hold your breath for a count of 7.
- Breathe out through your mouth for a count of 8, making a whooshing sound.
- Repeat four times.

If this exercise makes you light-headed, that is normal. Just stop, and the feeling should pass, and then you can resume or go more slowly. You are creating a greater oxygen flow to your body, which is a good thing, especially if you are a shallow breather, but it may take some getting used to.

Having these exercises at your disposal anytime and anywhere gives you a wonderful opportunity to "catch your breath" in the middle of caring for others. Each time you take advantage of taking a deep breath, you are treating yourself to a deep, relaxing pause. Instead of buzzing around barely breathing, you are taking it all in and then letting it all go.

Use Sleep As a Weapon

Getting enough sleep is probably the single most important self-care action caregivers can take. It recharges you, heals you, and builds up your immunity and stamina. Since sleep is such a vital part of being able to maintain your ability to be a balanced and strong caregiver, self-care around sleep is critical.

It may also be the hardest self-care activity to accomplish. Worry, stress, physical pain, and interruptions during the night from something urgent happening with your loved one can keep you from getting a good, solid night's sleep. You have to be proactive and focused on getting as much rest as possible. Take the following actions when preparing for bed so you are in optimal form to fall asleep as quickly and deeply as possible.

- **Put your phone down.** Leave your phone in another room or across the room if you need to have it on for emergency purposes. Long-distance caregivers who need to be available can leave the phone on but should not go to bed with the phone by their side. Putting your phone down and out of immediate reach allows you to turn off the part of your brain that is constantly scrolling, checking, and engaging. Plus, the blue screen stimulates you and makes you think it's daytime, so put it away!
- **If getting a good night's sleep continues to be difficult no matter what you do, grab rest and sleep whenever you can (and do not feel guilty about it).** You need sleep to survive, so get it anytime you can with pleasure! You are a better caregiver when you are rested.
- **Make your bedroom or the space you sleep in a place of rest and comfort.** Keep the temperature cool and keep it as quiet and dark as you can. Use clean, fresh sheets and scented pillows or pillows sprayed with scents such as lavender. Have this be a safe place you can unwind and sleep.
- **Sip and summarize.** Have a cup of caffeine-free tea. Adding milk and honey is not only delicious but both are said to help you feel sleepy.

Hopefully, you cut out any caffeine after lunch, so you won't be edgy. While sipping, celebrate the great job you did today.

- **If you are losing sleep because it's interrupted by your loved one and it's becoming a consistent issue, it's time to think about getting help.** Whether finding someone to spot you for a few nights so you can get caught up on sleep or adding someone to your team to stay nights, explore and discuss the possibilities. Reach out to your team to tackle the issue with you.

Sleep is not only a weapon; it's also a precious and an important caregiver ally. Guard your sleep time and don't give it away. The more you sleep, the healthier and happier you are. What better gift can you give to yourself and those you care for?

Create a Caregiver's Spa

Does caregiving have you worn-out and frazzled? Could you use a day at the spa? No time? No budget? Then make a spa at home and use it as often as you like! Any caregiver can make their bathroom into a spa retreat with a little imagination and creativity. Just like you make bathing as pleasant as possible for those you take care of, you can make your bathing time a relaxing getaway for yourself.

The next time you are grocery shopping for those you care for, take a detour down the personal care aisle. Here you will find the makings of the best spa in town. Check out the body wash section and find one that looks luxuriant and moisturizing. The most expensive is not always the best; your choice depends on what you find exciting. Check the ingredients and look for scents that you know you like and that will relax you. Buy a relaxing one and also one labeled as invigorating. That way you have a choice if you want to chill out or wake up!

Move over to the soaps and check out a scent that makes you close your eyes and say *ahhhhh*. Check out bath salts, bubbles, or bombs, and pick one that is soothing and one that is invigorating.

Now turn your attention to sponges. Loofahs are great for removing dead skin and stimulating your whole body. The mesh loofahs are great if you want a gentler sponge. They soap up well and give your skin a nice buff. When covered with body wash and soap, these sponges and loofahs lather up and make your whole body feel like it's on a vacation. The moisturizing body washes and soaps leave your skin feeling renewed. Back brushes are fun for those hard-to-reach spots. Also, don't forget the moisturizer! Grab a nice body lotion to finish off the glow!

Another important item to purchase for your home spa are towels. Every spa has thick, luxurious towels. Even if the budget is tight, invest in one comfy, high-absorption, luxury towel. You could even search online for an inexpensive quilted robe.

Claiming the space to enjoy your home spa includes setting the boundaries associated with taking "me time." Let those you care for and anyone else who needs to know that you plan to take this spa time and you are not to be disturbed. Enlist the help of others to take over for you if need be, and be clear they are not to invade your privacy. Be firm and stick to it. It may only be thirty or sixty minutes, but for that time, submerge yourself in relaxation and daydreams.

Savor Your Meals

Caregivers can often forget to eat. This activity is not only aimed at setting a reminder to eat regularly; it's also an incentive to take the time to actively savor and enjoy each part of the meal you have during your day.

Above and beyond the fact that eating a balanced, healthy meal helps fuel the caregiver body, enjoying the food you have prepared forces you to take a break from the busy caregiving whirlwind. By sitting down and appreciating your meal instead of rushing around gulping your food down, you are setting a tone for both your body and your mind that will help you relax and stay present in the moment. It will give you something to look forward to and allow you space to take a nice break while doing something essential for yourself. You won't skip as many meals if you view eating as a source of recharging and gratification.

Hopefully, you have gotten into the habit of setting a timer to remind yourself to have a healthy meal on a schedule. You can also plan to eat when you feed those you care for or when they are having their meals. This would be a good time for socialization, and you can set a powerful example by slowly enjoying your food to motivate them to do the same.

The next time you sit down to eat, try practicing these simple actions and helpful observations to make dining a pleasant activity.

- **Pause before beginning your meal and have a moment of appreciation and gratitude for the food.** Send up a prayer of thanks for this moment you've been given to stop and take care of yourself. Taking this time to check in puts your caregiving life in perspective and can give you much-needed respite.
- **Don't plan on doing anything other than eating your meal.** Put away the phone and any other chore you might normally try to do while you eat. Try to clear your mind. No multitasking, planning, or scheduling is allowed. You will concentrate only on your food.

- **Once you begin eating, don't rush.** Chew slowly, noticing each bite, savoring the taste, smell, and texture. Clear your mind of everything other than the food you are eating. Focus on your enjoyment of the food you are eating and stay completely present in the here and now.

When you savor your meals, you are slowing down and appreciating life. The caregiving responsibilities are on hold, and enjoyment is yours to own. This is an important type of action that signals your body, mind, and spirit that you care for yourself and are willing to take the time and energy to treat yourself with respect and love. When your meals become a ritual of thanksgiving, a space for relaxation, and staying in the moment with nothing else going on, you will be surprised how refreshed you will feel.

Moisturize

One of the most important things caregivers can do for those they care for, especially seniors, is to keep their skin moisturized. Especially in the winter months when cold weather and indoor heat pull the moisture out of the air, causing the skin to dry out.

Caregivers must moisturize as well. You, too, are exposed to elements, physical stressors, and dehydration. Using creams and lotions to fortify your skin is a great, proactive self-care activity that makes you feel good while it protects you.

Consider your skin type when you are looking for lotions and creams. Normal, dry, oily, sensitive, mature, or a combination of these dictates which moisturizers will work best for you. Creams, oils, and lotions do not have to be expensive; their ingredients are more important than the brand name.

You should wash regularly, but during the winter months it's wise to cut down the time you shower or bathe—especially if you have sensitive skin—so you retain as much moisture in your skin as possible. Lightly pat yourself dry to keep some moisture on your skin and apply your lotions and creams when your skin and face are still damp. This will trap the moisture in for best results. Make sure to apply any topical medication before you put on lotion or cream.

Since you are constantly washing your hands in your caregiving world and exposing them to harsh chemicals in hand sanitizers, make sure you have soothing, healing hand lotion everywhere you wash your hands so you can apply it right after washing your hands.

Practice Mindfulness with the Five Senses

There's so much talk about how mindfulness is helpful for caregivers. Mindfulness is simply the ability to focus on, pay attention to, and stay in the present moment, instead of planning, worrying, projecting into the future, or beating yourself up for the past. Practicing mindfulness can help any caregiver face their role with a feeling of calm fulfillment.

Try this "five senses" mindfulness exercise to learn how to create a state of mindfulness you can visit whenever you want. It helps you tune in to your surroundings and environment and direct your attention to the present. Practice it as often as possible so it becomes a part of your healthy self-care routine.

1. Sit down in a quiet space and take a few breaths. Look around you and notice five things you can see. Pick things that stand out or things you wouldn't normally notice.

2. Now notice four things that you can feel. Be aware of the chair you are sitting in or how your feet feel or your heartbeat.

3. Now become aware of three things you can hear, such as the rustling of leaves in the wind or the traffic.

4. Now become aware of two things you can smell.

5. Finally, notice one thing you can taste. Have a cup of tea or a healthy snack waiting for this step.

Running through this exercise can settle you down and allow you to get back into your caregiving day refreshed and with a less busy mind.

Watch Out for Exertion/Exhaustion

Every caregiver knows that life is about balance. While never easy to maintain, balance is about pacing and awareness. Maintaining balance in all you do guides you to a healthier body and mind. Looking out for trouble spots or patterns of behavior that pull you out of balance will help to identify things you do that hurt you and throw you off. You can then make positive changes around the harmful things you do and get back on track.

One of the most common trouble spots of caregiving is exertion/exhaustion. This is a behavioral pattern of overworking and then paying the price with utter exhaustion to the point where everything is overwhelming, and you stop being productive.

In an effort to be all things to all people and fix everything, caregivers fall into the trap of exertion/exhaustion. The need to prove to everyone, especially yourself, that you are a capable caregiver coupled with the heavy burden of responsibility you bear making sure those you care for are comfortable and sound contributes to this self-defeating syndrome.

Caregivers can begin to change this pattern by being aware that they are susceptible to the habit of pushing themselves too hard and paying close attention to why and when they do it, stopping it before it's too late.

Start by being realistic about what you can and cannot do. You can't do it all, and you can't do it all at once. No one expects you to be perfect or some kind of magician. Caregiving is just as effective when it's calm and consistent. Taking steady, small steps is a great way to chisel away at things. Make a plan, and be realistic about how to build these small steps into big results so you don't overdo it. You can always delegate, and there's always tomorrow.

Taking breaks is effective and efficient. Plan break times for yourself. No matter where you are in your day, put down what you're doing for a few minutes. Walk away, stretch, snack, do something that clears your mind and refreshes you. Taking a break before you are too tired makes you more productive because you have renewed energy. You are operating at optimum energy instead of being depleted.

If you forget to take some breaks and get caught up in a whirlwind of activity and all of a sudden feel tired or overwhelmed, stop. Address the red flags your body is showing you and respond accordingly. Put the task to the side for another day. You have overdone it and are on the brink of exhaustion. Next time you'll do better and catch yourself before it's too late.

Exertion/exhaustion can be avoided with practice and perseverance, and balance can always be restored.

Use Grounding Techniques to Alleviate Anxiety

It's common for caregivers to feel anxious or worried. Help yourself feel less anxious and more in balance by using grounding techniques that make you more aware of the present moment, your surroundings, and what's going on in your body and mind.

Here are several grounding techniques you can use anytime you need to get grounded and calm.

- **If you are lucky enough to have a pet, your furry friend can act like a magic grounding machine.** Pet them and pay attention to how they are responding. Notice how their fur and body feel as you run your hand over them. Feel the love you have for each other.
- **You can try repeating a grounding phrase or affirmation for a minute or so.** The most effective type of phrase is a personal mantra you design for yourself. For instance, repeat, "Good job! I'm proud of me for all that I have done today and every day." Or "I am safe and a good person." Personalize these affirmations and add anything that makes you feel safe and comforted.
- **Take a moment to sit quietly and visualize your favorite day at the beach or in nature, and try to remember as many small details as possible.** Feel the wind, hear the birds. Relax and unwind.

You can invent other grounding techniques that have a more personal stamp. Whatever you choose, apply these techniques the minute you feel anxious. They will calm you down and redirect your energy to feeling hopeful and ready for action.

Chapter 3: Self-Care for Your Spirit and Soul

Caregivers are often hardwired to have concern for others. Even if you show up reluctantly in the beginning, you usually have compassion and feel the need to make a difference in the world and be there for those who need help or can't take care of themselves. You never question the commitment or challenge of the caregiving role or the need to do it. You are in for the long haul and would never think of quitting, even when it becomes tough to do the job.

Caring for your own heart and soul during the caregiving experience is the only way to stay strong during the many storms that will rage around you. The same compassion, kindness, and generosity you shower on those you care for must also be given to yourself.

In this chapter, you will find simple actions you can take to love and appreciate yourself and the caregiving you do. You will learn to schedule time to nurture your spirit and soul. These actions are as straightforward as practicing breathing exercises and sitting in the sun and as uncomplicated as claiming fifteen minutes to do something that gives you joy. Permitting yourself to prioritize your spiritual needs is integral to being whole and happy.

When you fill up your emotional bank account by nourishing your heart and soul, you can draw on that account to remain serene, balanced, and grounded no matter what challenges you face as a caregiver. Enjoy these self-care activities geared to nurturing your spirit as you work to uplift the spirits of others.

Meditate

There are many ways to meditate—it all depends on how much time you have and what works best for you. Taking five or ten minutes daily to sit quietly away from the hustle and bustle of caregiving helps to center you. You could even check out free classes at your public library, hospital, or community center, and on *YouTube*.

Here are some basic tips you might try:

- Find a quiet place. Keep this place as your special sanctuary.
- Set a timer for five, ten, or fifteen minutes, or any amount of time you feel works for you.
- Sit comfortably in an alert but relaxed position.
- Concentrate by focusing on your breathing or repeating a positive word or phrase.

Know that your mind will race and thoughts like "Am I doing this right?" or even "I forgot to get oatmeal!" will bombard you. This is normal. Just try to think of these thoughts as cars driving by and go back to listening to your breath or repeating your phrase.

There is no goal in meditation other than having quiet time so you can catch your breath and take a break. Meditation is the perfect way to decompress from the demands and stress of caregiving, and when practiced as often as possible, it can help avoid caregiver burnout. It's like a mini-vacation that keeps you balanced. It relaxes your body and helps to clear all the conversations, doubts, and worries out of your mind.

Don't Do It Alone

You can be a conductor, but you can't play all the instruments! You need other caregivers to help you play your symphony. You may feel safer and less vulnerable being a lone wolf, but you cannot do this alone. Caregiving takes a village.

Even if you are a loner by nature, caregiving changes everything. While you might have been used to doing things on your own for most of your life, you are now in a situation that requires you to be part of a team. You are not only responsible for yourself; you are also responsible for the well-being of others. They are the ones who will suffer the most if you stubbornly insist on trying to weather the storm on your own.

Ask yourself why you feel safer alone and what fears you might have about involving other people. Is it because you are afraid of what they might think of you? Is it because you feel as though you have failed if you can't hack it alone?

Make it a point to discuss this with people you trust so you get feedback and support. Seek professional help if you feel you need extra support. By addressing the fears or issues that make you hesitate to reach out for help, you are starting a process that will allow you to stop isolating and enjoy the relief of letting others share the burden of responsibility.

Reward Yourself Once a Day

Once a day, ring the bell! Figuratively and literally if that makes it more fun! Nothing is nicer than rewarding yourself during your caregiving duties. Not only does it feel great; it's also well deserved and appropriate!

You may not feel like jumping up and down with joy; in fact, you may feel like throwing the towel in, but that makes it even more important that you stop what you are doing and reward yourself for just showing up in your role as a caregiver. Showing up is a big deal.

Taking a few minutes to reward yourself makes you feel better in the moment and positive about your day. You can always include those you care for in this activity, especially if the reward is a cookie or two or a great cup of tea or coffee. Or both! This could be a great way to get fluids in your loved one and take a quick break yourself.

Forget about needing a reason for a reward; you get a reward just because you are a caregiver. That selfless, compassionate, outstanding decision needs to be celebrated every day. If you are the guilty type and feel like you need a tangible reason for a reward, then write down one thing you pulled off today. If more than one accomplishment comes to mind, add that! Good job! You are amazing! Enjoy that well-deserved reward!

Honor and Respect Others

So many of the pitfalls you face as a caregiver can be avoided by using, having, and showing respect. Not only for those you care for but for the people you encounter daily as well.

We all love to be acknowledged, heard, and supported. By clearly letting others know how much you respect them and wish to hear and support them, you set the tone for your interaction with them. It starts everything off on the right foot and will continue to make your relationships with those you care for and everyone you encounter richer and mutually enjoyable.

Being mindful of how you are treating others and taking the time to check your attitude, frustration, and any other side effect of caregiving at the door before you meet with someone guarantees rewarding interactions instead of upsetting or uncomfortable ones. Focus on the person right in front of you, not a grouch you just encountered.

Respect requires effort and is easier to find when you know and understand the lives of those you interact with. Encourage those you care for to talk about their lives by asking them questions with true interest and curiosity. Find out what makes them tick. Show interest in the nurses, doctors, healthcare providers, customer service reps, and anyone you work with. Once you get to know someone, what they've been through, and all the things you have in common, you gain a deeper respect for them. They will notice and return the honor.

Be Grateful

Gratitude can be a lifesaver. It's a miracle waiting to happen. It can change your mood and attitude within seconds. Having gratitude can take you out of your pity party, soothe your fears, destroy your resentments, and give you hope and faith.

Caregivers have an edge when it comes to looking for gratitude. No one understands the fragility of life and how short it is more than caregivers do. Every day you see the precious and fleeting nature of life. It's where your desperation to fix everything comes from and also your desire to cherish each day. It's this ability to appreciate and be grateful that you need to focus on. Try the following activities to find gratitude and to appreciate the gifts of positivity and possibility it can bring you.

- **Write a gratitude list.** Of all the endless lists you have in your caregiving life, this one benefits you emotionally and spiritually. Write down three things you are grateful for. Add more if you wish. Save this list and keep it somewhere that is easy to see, and refer to it often. You can even make a new list every day or any time you need to. Listing the things you have, or the moments of joy with those you love, or something that reminds you of the goodness of your life can be an eye-opener. It's a positive reality check.

- **Appreciate your loved ones.** Take the time to appreciate those you care for. Think about what they mean to you and how they have influenced your life. See their bravery. What will be lost when they are gone? Notice the love and gratitude they have for you even if it's only a little smile at times. Hold on to that smile and any other special moments you have with them.

- **Surround yourself with other grateful people.** Gratitude is contagious. Surround yourself with people who see the good in life and the lessons in challenges; those who think miracles exist and consider themselves lucky to be alive. When you are in the company of grateful people, the world becomes brighter.

- **Take stock of your caregiving experience.** Even the most frustrating or heartbreaking caregiving experience brings with it extraordinary gifts. Learning about yourself, getting to know those you care for on a deeper basis, healing relationships, or simply finding courage or strength you never knew you had are all part of the equation. Take an inventory of the changes you experienced during your journey. There will always be something to be grateful for.

Gratitude changes your perspective and helps you see the good stuff. It reminds you that you are only on this caregiving journey once and that even in the darkest hours there are things you are blessed with that you may never have again.

Remember This Is Temporary

This, too, shall pass. That may be hard for caregivers to relate to at 2:00 in the morning when the walls feel like they are closing in and the fear that those you care for are sick and suffering and you are not doing enough to give them comfort is haunting you and preventing you from sleeping. When you are stuck in the nightmare of thinking things will be like this forever and there is no way out or no solution, it can be hard to find comfort.

At times like this you must remember that nothing lasts forever. Not even the darkest hour. Change is always around the corner. That's one consistent thing about caregiving, it's always changing.

By reminding yourself that what you are facing or going through is temporary, you can find the perspective you need and even find hope that what is coming next will be so much better for you. Remember other times when you felt like you couldn't go on, but you did anyway and things improved.

Get your support team on board by sharing how you are feeling with them and discuss all the times you felt like you were in caregiver quicksand in the past and how things ended up working out and you survived. Nothing lasts forever, and everything is temporary. Even the good stuff. Hang in there.

Pet Your Pet

Animals are magical when it comes to creating joy and comfort and adding lots of unconditional love—and for caregivers, they can be a lifeline. Pets can show you how uncomplicated and happy life can be just by wagging their tails or meowing when they see you. They always let you know how special they think you are and shower you with love and affection.

Spending quality time petting and playing with your pet and getting that unconditional love from them can turn a whole day around—or at least make whatever is bothering you bearable or even forgotten for a few minutes. If you are feeling defeated or unappreciated, go pet your cat or dog, throw a ball, or take a walk with them. Let them show you love, how to have some fun, and how staying in the moment is the way to live.

If you don't have a pet, investigate local pet therapy programs. These programs have specially trained dogs (who study hard to get their official therapy dog vests) and other animals that travel to facilities and institutions for the day and may even be able to come to your home. This is a spectacular outlet for anyone you care for and you can get lots of petting and hugging time in for yourself too. Let your furry friends remind you that everything will be okay as long as there's food, treats, snoozing, and love!

Journal about Caregiving

One of the ways caregivers can alleviate stress and unwind from the emotional turmoil and upheaval they face daily is to write about it. Something happens when you put pen to paper and write down what you are feeling, what happened during your day, and any thoughts that keep circling in your head. Keeping a journal can be a wonderful outlet for all the big feelings caregiving triggers. It can alleviate stress and worry, clear your mind, help you find new perspectives, and give you a chance to let off steam.

If you've never kept a journal, now is the time to start one. If you have journaled before, you know how helpful it can be. There is no right or wrong way to journal, and no special book or tablet is required. Your journal is for you and you only; no one else needs to see it. Use this journal to write about how tired or angry or frustrated caregiving makes you.

Write about challenges you are facing and how difficult it is to stay positive and kind with those you love and care for when you are exhausted and feel like you can't fix them or yourself. There doesn't have to be a structure to your journal, and you can add anything you want, such as drawings or doodling. This is about what you are going through, how your caregiving role makes you feel, and what you are thinking.

Start small and find a groove. Just write a little here and there. Test it out. You might journal before bed or at random times during the day when you need to let off steam. You can do this every day or wait until the urge hits you. It's a great way to pass time while waiting in doctors' waiting rooms or when you are on hold for what seems like hours with the health insurance company.

Start anywhere. Be honest and open. Just let the words flow and the feelings be expressed. Ask questions, debate, let loose, and scream on paper. Tell the universe how angry you are that your loved ones aren't getting better and that it isn't fair. Let the grief flow and anger erupt. Write down the good stuff and memories you are making during your caregiving journey, and talk about the joy too. Write a novel or just a sentence. This is not about being a great writer or winning a prize or setting any goals. This is a space where your inner caregiver can let it all hang out and not be judged or criticized by anyone.

This is a memoir for one. Caregiving is an intense, big, powerful experience, and writing about it and capturing even a small bit of it can be so healing. Once you try this amazing self-care tool, it can become a solid source of relief and even wonder. You might be surprised at the brave, special person you begin to see in those pages.

Manage Your Time on Social Media

There are wonderful places to connect with other caregivers on the Internet. You can find *Facebook* groups and caregiving communities that share general issues or ones that cover specific conditions such as Parkinson's or Alzheimer's. These groups offer a unique and supportive place to share your caregiving story, vent, ask questions, and reach out. As with anything on the Internet, always vet any group you think might be right for you before you join to make sure it's a legitimate and properly monitored space.

This type of interaction can be comforting, supportive, and a good use of social media. As a caregiver, you can't always get away from those you serve to join caregiver support groups in your area, so social media, which is available 24/7, offers a great alternative and can be a wonderful way to avoid isolation. For this purpose, when used wisely, these resources are valuable and positive.

Sadly, not all social media is positive and safe, and caregivers need to be careful and sensible when it comes to using it. It's one thing to find groups that are supportive and relatable; it's another to try to find escape in apps or platforms that don't have your best interests at heart or make you feel bad about yourself and your life.

If you tend to lean toward sites that show everyone living their best lives on a beach or allow and encourage negative messages or comments, you may be asking for trouble. The last thing you need to be doing is comparing and despairing or posting something on a platform that allows criticism or meanness to thrive. Why would you want to waste your precious moments of downtime to look at negative comments or posts that aren't supportive?

There are two simple ways to tell if your social media usage is healthy, balanced, and worthwhile.

- **Check in with yourself.** How does this platform make you feel? When you are on your favorite place on social media, do you feel supported, heard, and right with the world? Or do you feel down or bad or unsettled?

If you feel worse than when you started, get off that platform and stay off it. It's never going to get better. You are wasting time that could be used for other healthy activities.

- **Watch how often and how long you are online.** Are you spending more time on social media than you allowed or bargained for? It can be addicting. Try timing yourself and see if you feel satisfied and enjoyed scrolling for that allocated time. You can always schedule another session. But if you feel like you are going down a black hole with no end in sight, it may be time to find another outlet like reading or knitting to give you pleasure.

Like everything in life, moderation is always the best policy. Social media can be a great resource for caregivers to connect with like-minded friends, or it can become a time destroyer. Be smart and manage your social media time wisely.

Give Yourself a Parade

There are lots of ongoing issues and long, drawn-out solutions in caregiving. While there may be quick fixes occasionally, usually it takes a series of phone calls over numerous days, multiple agencies or healthcare providers to deal with, lots of research, and trial and error with new meds or apparatuses. All of which requires grit and persistence.

Caregivers become tenacious and unstoppable in the name of caregiving, and you can take for granted how courageous and hard that is. You get so used to working tirelessly to right a wrong or fix a problem that when you finally get something resolved, you don't stop to appreciate the fact that you've been so successful.

Don't let this success go unnoticed! Give yourself a parade! Literally! Go to *YouTube* on your phone, tablet, or TV; look for the highest-energy marching band on there; turn up the volume as loud as it goes; and play the video! March around like a star! Get those you work with or take care of to join in. Everyone loves a parade!

Doing fun, upbeat, and positive things like giving yourself a parade takes five minutes out of your day, but it can clear the air and remind you to honor all the hard work you do every day. It celebrates how much you accomplish by your persistence and care. If you get in the habit of giving yourself a parade when you deserve one, you will be flexing those all-important self-appreciation muscles. So get out your baton!

Pick Your Battles

All caregivers face resistance from those they care for at some point. Role reversal, pain, frustration, lack of stimulation or too much of it, anxiety, and fear are just some of the reasons those you care for can be difficult or resist what is good for them.

Trying to get your loved one to cooperate for things like showering or eating or taking medications when you are constantly met with an argument can make you want to pull your hair out and go screaming into the night.

You need to pick your battles. If you want peace and serenity, you need to choose the most pressing issues to go to battle with and walk away from the rest. You can always approach those issues later.

Ask yourself this very strategic question when you hit the wall of resistance and those you care for start to dig in their heels: "How important is it?" In the big scheme of things, how important is this thing you are about to go to battle for? Is it worth engaging in what could potentially be a knockdown fight?

If the answer is that it's not very important at all, let the issue go, retreat, take the high road, smile, and back away. By carefully picking your battles, you are left with the energy to negotiate when there's a much more critical win you need down the road. If it's not that important, nix it.

Play Your Favorite Music and Sing

We all have our favorite music and songs that can give us joy, bring back memories, and soothe us through difficult times. When caregiving feels hopeless, music can inject joy back into your life, so go put your records on!

Studies have shown that music activates an area of the brain that stimulates communication and pleasure, and can even improve memory. Research also suggests that music can improve cognitive function and quality of life in some people with Alzheimer's and dementia, and the results are quite amazing.

Play music as often as you can throughout the day, even before bed. Find music that is soothing to the environment if your loved one is overly sensitive. Soft, gentle music can be effective, depending on the situation. If it's not disturbing to those you care for, find uplifting, fun, happy, up-tempo songs. Find a playlist on **Spotify**, ask Alexa to pick some tunes, or listen to your favorite radio station. Your loved one can give you some suggestions too! If you are lucky enough that those you care for can join the listening fest, it can become a wonderful shared experience.

If your environment needs to be quiet and unstimulating for those you care for, invest in headphones or earphones for those times when you can use them to listen to music and still pay attention to everything that is going on.

When the time is right, crank up the music, get the hairbrush out, and sing along even if you have to lip-sync. Smiles are guaranteed.

Sit in the Sun

Doing something as simple as sitting in the sun can be extremely difficult for caregivers. Enjoying this quiet, lovely pleasure is often put on hold (along with many other self-care activities) because caregiving has you focused on so many other serious issues.

The reality is that when you stop doing and enjoying activities like taking five to ten minutes to sit in the sun and just soak it in, you are upping the probability that you will be more stressed and more likely to experience caregiver burnout.

It's been proven that taking breaks during the workday helps employees be more efficient and creative, and it restores energy. If this works for a normal nine-to-five workday, it should definitely be applied to the long haul of caregiving!

It doesn't pay to deny yourself self-care and pleasure. When you don't break up your day or allow yourself some brief downtime, everybody suffers. You feel more tired and resentful, and therefore you are a less enthusiastic caregiver.

So go ahead. Do yourself and everyone else a favor. Get some vitamin D. Go sit in the sun. Close your eyes, put your face up, and let the sun shine down on it. Don't feel guilty about doing it; in fact, feel guilty about *not* doing it!

Live Just for Today

Sometimes you can get so overwhelmed by the big picture of caregiving that all the planning and strategizing can seem endless. It begins to feel as though you have taken on an impossible mission. Seeing the light at the end of the very long tunnel getting smaller and farther away feels discouraging. Often your caregiving role can seem much bigger than you are.

All caregivers struggle with this discouraging feeling, but help can be found by remembering that the only thing you need to do is just get through today. You don't have to worry about tomorrow or the day after; you only need to worry about today and how you can show up for the next twenty-four hours. You can do anything if it's just for one day. You don't have to do anything forever; you only have to do it for today.

When problems feel endless or chores and tasks seem to stretch on forever, let yourself off the hook for anything other than what you need to do today. Use "just for today" as a mantra. Every time you feel nervous or begin to project into the future, repeat "just for today, just for today." Say it out loud if you need to! Write "Just for today" on a sticky note on your mirror so you see it first thing in the morning and all day long. No regrets about yesterday and no worries about tomorrow. You live "just for today."

Enjoy an Occasional Ice Cream Splurge

Overindulging in cakes, cookies, ice cream, or chocolate as your caregiving day becomes hard and those you care for become difficult is not a recipe for a successful day. Your glucose levels will most likely spike, then drop, and then your moment of pleasure might end up making you feel worse than you did before you overdid it.

Moderation is key, however, and an occasional small scoop of ice cream or a piece of dark chocolate when you need a treat is fine. Really. Of course, be smart and careful and don't let stress make you do crazy things to get relief, but for Pete's sake, safely indulge occasionally! It's okay. And if you do overdo it, relax. That's okay too.

Self-care for caregivers is about treating yourself to little celebrations, tiny breaks, pieces of chocolate, and self-forgiveness. If a treat can make you sigh and smile, then go for it; you deserve it. And if you overdo it, you also deserve to say, hey, that's okay. Let's be better next time.

Go Float Your Boat

When you are busy running around calling doctors, shopping, following up on insurance claims, fixing dinner, and dispensing meds, doing things that make you happy can sometimes get lost in the shuffle.

Doing something that gives you joy, floats your boat, and makes you feel fulfilled and happy can recharge you and help you to feel reconnected to your own life, likes, and desires. This connection is vital if you want to remain a happy, healthy caregiver.

Do you have a hobby? Do you have a favorite TV show? Do you have a bench to sit on? Do you have a favorite cup of tea and cookie? Is there a book you've been dying to read? When was the last time you did a crossword puzzle or got out the crafts, paints, watercolors, coloring book, or card game?

Plan a time right now to take thirty minutes this week to get your boat out and float in it. Put a time on the calendar and, if need be, move the date around but do not put it off until next week. Set a timer for thirty minutes once you sit down and do not get up unless it's an emergency. Turn the phone off and give in to the joy of doing something you love for a full thirty minutes. The result may not hit you right away, but once you get into a groove every week, this special "you time" will keep you refreshed and more grounded.

Establish an End-of-Day Ritual

After a long, tiring day as a caregiver, all you may want to do is find some peace and quiet, and relax. You deserve it, you need it, and, if you can pull it off, it's not only a miracle; it's heaven!

Set up this precious time at the end of your day to be as rewarding as possible. Take a few minutes to reflect on your day and accomplishments, and make note of your intentions for tomorrow. Adding a quick, easy little ritual to this well-deserved downtime can make it even more enjoyable and productive.

Grab a pen and paper or notebook and jot down all the things you accomplished and knocked out of the park today. Start with getting up and showing up. Don't be surprised if the list is longer than you expected. Caregivers never realize how much they do in a day.

After telling yourself "good job," think about tomorrow and the things you must do and then add in things you'd love to do. Don't forget to add at least one self-care activity. This doesn't have to take a lot of thought or energy; it's just a quick list of intentions. Now you can relax and sleep without worrying about tomorrow or thinking about today in terms of what didn't get done. You have congratulated yourself for your successes and have a schedule for tomorrow. Now your brain can turn off, and so can you!

Hit the Restart Button

Once your caregiving day begins and you are off and running to doctors' offices or setting up medications or making appointments, you hope the day will go along as planned, even though it's rare that things in the caregiving world ever go as planned!

To break this habit of being frustrated and annoyed when things go off track, you can hit the restart button anytime during the day. When you are so frustrated or angry that it feels like steam might start coming out of your ears, put everything down and stop what you are doing. Think of a big red button that says "restart" on it and hit it in your mind.

Then do one simple thing that shakes things up. Hug your loved one. Do a silly dance. Go get some cookies and share them with someone. Get some fresh air. Go to the restroom or step outside of the doctor's office into the sunshine for a moment. Tell a joke or ask someone else what their favorite joke is. Now you can return to whatever you were doing and start over.

Taking ten minutes to switch it all up and take a little break from the day you are trying to plow through helps you to hit the restart button and begin again. And remember, there are no limits on how many times that button gets used in a day!

Be Kind to Yourself

Caregivers are experts at spreading love and kindness to others from what seems like an unlimited source. Sadly, this kindness is usually directed outward instead of inward, where it may be needed the most. Even the most experienced caregiver must remember that self-kindness, one of the most empowering caregiver tools there is, must be practiced. You need to actively work at treating yourself as kindly as you treat those you care for. Here are some ideas you can try:

- At least once a day, try to say a kind or gentle word to yourself about how special you are. Stop beating yourself up about your unintentional mistakes and acknowledge how hard you try. You need to recognize what a good person you are.
- Try writing down one thing about yourself that makes you lovable or awesome, or a unique way you tried your best, or an amazing compliment someone gave you.
- Make note of your kindness to others and promise to extend some to yourself. When you do something that makes someone's day better, stop and tell yourself that you are generous and that's why you shine.

Finally, when something seems to go wrong or feels like a failure, treat yourself to the kind and gentle forgiveness you would give to someone else when they tried their very best but didn't quite hit the mark. Shower yourself with the same kindness and respect you so easily give to others. You deserve it.

Celebrate Small Victories

Caregivers need to celebrate their small victories. The tendency to quickly plow ahead from one pressing thing to another is understandable, but pausing to praise the great job you just did and to appreciate what you've accomplished can energize and inspire you.

Actions, even the small ones, add up, and before you know it, a problem has been solved, a question has been answered, or you have gotten the response you needed. Each time you make something happen or work on making something better as a caregiver, you need to acknowledge your strength and courage to work on a solution even when you are exhausted. Put up sticky notes that say "celebrate" where you can see them during the day, so you are reminded to stop and take a victory lap in your mind for the small triumphs.

Try not to take even your smallest efforts for granted. Pause and say a little prayer of gratitude for the strength you receive to be able to power through your caregiving day. Not everything in caregiving is going to be a big win or move a big mountain. The big wins only happen by adding up the little ones. Thank yourself for always trying to make it all work, celebrate all the actions you take, and own all your victories, big and little.

Stop Worrying about What Others Think

When we are young, we are taught to be concerned about the opinions of others. While what other people think may be interesting, it should never influence you or matter more than your own intuitive knowing. Caregivers can fall into this dangerous trap of worrying about how they appear to others and how they might be judged for the job they are doing. It's one thing to receive suggestions or positive feedback, but worrying about or letting the opinions of others affect your caregiving decisions is self-defeating and foolish. What other people think of you is none of your business.

Remember, you are not a mind reader. You have no idea what anyone else is thinking unless they tell you. If someone does speak up and offers criticism, talk to them about it. It can be a great opportunity to get a new perspective or see things through someone else's eyes. Be open to learning something if it's constructive, but nip it in the bud if it's inappropriate or unjustified by thanking them for their suggestions and changing the subject. Good, supportive conversation and suggestions should always be welcome, but judgment isn't allowed. Not everyone may agree on your caregiving style. But if you are acting with love and good intention, no one else needs to give you approval, nor do you need it from them. The opinion in your heart is the only one that matters, and it's the only one you need to listen to.

Let Go of Control

Are you hovering over everyone and everything? Being a helicopter caregiver can feel like the right strategy. There is so much going on, many people to manage, a lot to organize, and an enormous number of tasks to accomplish.

Keeping control over the chaos and challenges of caregiving is indeed important, and type-A personalities who command control tend to handle the stress of caregiving well. However, trying to exert control over everyone and everything not only takes a tremendous amount of energy; it can also put everyone else on edge, especially those you care for and work with. It can create a rigidity that isn't always productive.

If everything must be "my way or the highway," you need to take a good look in the mirror and make some personality adjustments right away. You are not the only one who can do it perfectly, make it work, or get it right. You need to let go of control.

Letting go of control is never easy. Ironically, however, trying to control everything often makes the situation worse and everyone around you miserable. Nothing goes smoothly, and it's exhausting. Consider these tips when it starts to become obvious that being a helicopter caregiver is getting you nowhere and you feel exhausted.

- **Check on your motives.** What's really behind your need to control everything and everybody? Fear? Perfectionism? What would happen if you let go of control? What's the worst-case scenario and the best? Your need to control usually comes from the worry that things will be disastrous and you will fail. This is a limiting and unrealistic way to view your world, and it has no basis in reality. Get out of this mindset.
- **Delegate.** Since it's not feasible that you can do it all alone, you can delegate things to other people. Have someone do the shopping or take those you care for outside for fresh air or feed them lunch. Don't

micromanage. Once you've delegated tasks and activities to others, let them do it their way and leave them alone! When you begin to see that the sky isn't going to fall and it feels good to have help, you will relax a little.

Try trusting that everything is going to be okay by letting go of small things first to see what happens if you don't do everything your way. You really can't control anything other than your own actions and reactions, so you need to stop hovering and let it all go.

Get Rid of the Judge in Your Head

We all have a judge and jury in our heads. We all know it's not kind or productive, yet we engage in judging ourselves and others. One would think that caregivers get a free pass and don't have to join the self-judgment party since they are selfless and committed to serving others. But most caregivers are guilty of the same negative self-criticism everyone experiences.

Being self-critical is a nasty habit, and it's destructive. It's one thing to analyze a situation so changes can be made; it's another to beat yourself up and be unforgiving. Beating yourself up doesn't create a solution; instead, it's debilitating. We all make mistakes, and we are all afraid of failing. Although the stakes are high in your caregiving role, if you are showing up for the job, you are already a superstar and doing more than most.

Here are some guidelines to getting rid of that judge and jury in your head:

- **Be on the lookout for your inner critic.** You must first be aware of the fact you are judging yourself and feel it in action. What are you saying to yourself? Are you questioning your caregiving abilities? Are you giving yourself a hard time? You might be surprised at how often you are doing this. Shine a light on judging yourself to clean it up. The faster you catch yourself doing it, the faster you can work to make it stop.
- **Argue with that judging voice in your head.** Talk back to self-criticism. Go over all the great things you did for your loved ones today and tell yourself you are not a failure; you are a pro doing a great job! Point out all the things you accomplished. Tell yourself that the bad things you are saying to yourself are simply not true and you refuse to listen.
- **Instead of judging or criticizing, try being kind, gentle, and supportive to yourself.** Replace the nasty stuff with positive, supportive comments. Tell yourself, "Good job, I'm proud of me for everything I did

today. I'm a superstar caregiver and the universe agrees! I'm so blessed to be who I am!"

- **Discuss self-criticism with others.** Open up to other caregivers in your tribe about the things bouncing around in your head. Not only will they give you positive feedback about how you are doing; they will also be the first ones to admit they, too, have an inner judge and jury to contend with!

Many people like to beat themselves up, but you don't have to go to that party! Self-criticism only works if you put up with it. Give it up and show the judge and jury the door.

Laugh!

Laughter is magical. When you laugh, everything looks better. It puts you in a good mood, it positively changes your brain chemistry, and it gives you a break from the cares of the world around you. No one needs or appreciates laughter more than caregivers. Laughter is a healing and special self-care tool for caregivers. It helps you survive the worst times and underscores the most memorable times in your caregiving journey.

There will be times in your caregiving life that are sad and all-consuming, and it can be difficult to find your sense of humor. It can sometimes feel as though you will never laugh again. To pull yourself out of this dark place, you need to get in touch with your funny bone. Doing so can make the difference between a bad day and a good one. Finding the funny needs to be a priority for you. Here are a few tips to help get your laughter back:

- **Create a reason to laugh.** *YouTube* and *TikTok* feature outlandish laugh-producing performances. Cat videos or goats in pajamas alone can offer lots of opportunities to turn on the smiles and laughs. We all think different things are funny, but between social media, TV, and films we can all find and watch something that makes us laugh out loud. Find your favorite and watch it whenever you can—and often. Include those you care for. They need laughter too!
- **Use your imagination.** When something bad happens or during your least favorite caregiving chores, use your imagination to try to picture clowns running around you or come up with some other goofy image that makes you see the absurdity of some of the things you have to do as a caregiver. There are some things no one (other than other caregivers) would believe you are reduced to doing. Try to see the humor in it all.
- **Call or hang out with funny people.** We all have that family member or friend who makes us laugh out loud. Spend a few minutes with them. If

nothing is tickling your funny bone, reminisce about a time when you both laughed so hard you cried. As you go over and remember the details, the laughs and giggles will start up before you know it. There's nothing like a shared funny experience.

Anything silly and funny is not only good for you; it's also good for everyone. Laughter has a healing, upbeat energy and communicates fun and safety even to those who can't understand what's going on. They can feel laughter and know that things are going to be okay because laughter makes everything feel right with the world. Cherish laughter and do it often.

Begin Your Day Expecting Miracles

Caregivers know that miracles happen because most of them experience at least one miracle in their caregiving journey. Most caregivers will experience a feeling of hopelessness at least once or twice as they care for their loved ones only to be surprised by something that saves the day or makes things better. Miracles can happen, and it helps if you believe in them and invite them to appear.

Starting your day expecting miracles is a great way to invite them into your life. Instead of giving in to the feeling of impending doom or worry when you wake up, you can tell yourself that this new day holds promise, and a miracle might find you today. You have a choice when you start each day: You can either envision difficulty and expect a rough time, or you can take a moment before you jump out of bed to send up a prayer or request that this day will hold surprises and possibilities. It's inspirational to take a moment before you start racing around to get quiet and ask God, or the universe, or any higher power you believe in to send you some grace and the ability to remember how important you are, not only to those you serve but to the world. Since you deserve every miracle that's coming to you, ask to see one today. Always expect miracles because that's when they happen.

Zip Your Lips

You have an answer for everything. It's your job as a caregiver. You are supposed to have answers. It's what makes you so good at managing the lives of those who need your help to survive and thrive. Your answers and feedback might not always be welcome, however. There are times when you should refrain from speaking up and instead zip your lips.

Knowing when and how to do this is an art that develops with effort and time. It's a perfect tactic to have at your disposal when communicating with those you care for. It forces you to listen to them instead of the sound of your own voice. You not only gain insight from what you are hearing; you are also proactively creating space for better conversation and a more relaxing environment.

If you see someone's eyes glazing over as you are speaking or they start to look annoyed, bored, or angry, it's time to put this great little tool into practice.

Ask yourself the following questions when you feel like you are talking too much, too fast, or too inappropriately: "Does this need to be said, does it need to be said now, and does it need to be said by me?" Answer honestly, and if you need to, zip those lips. Zipping your lips is a secret weapon that helps avoid conflict and encourages positive conversation with those you serve and work with.

Regain Your Balance

Imagine you are riding a horse. You are riding down a path and trying to stick to the middle of the road. It feels good to be going calmly, straight down the middle. The horse will sometimes get distracted and veer off to the right, and you will have to gently guide it back to the middle and continue on your way. The horse will once again get distracted and veer to the left, and you once again will gently guide it back to the middle. The middle is where the balance is.

Caregiving is constantly pulling you this way and that way, moving you away from the balance you work so hard to keep. Just like you would gently guide that horse back to the middle of the road, you need to gently guide yourself back to your balance.

Realize you always have a choice. You can stay out of sync, or you can snap out of it and try to get your balance back. It's not your fault if you get off balance, but if you stay there, that's on you. You can get back in the middle of the road by trying every self-care trick in this book until one of them works and you start to feel balanced. You need to work at being balanced, and self-awareness is the key.

Being honest with yourself about what has you thrown off balance is a great way to reclaim your stability. This can be anything in your caregiving life that makes you anxious or procrastinate or fills you with dread. Be on the lookout for these feelings and take the time to notice them. Write about your feelings and think about why you feel this way. Can you come up with a plan that allows someone else to carry out these tasks or show up for these situations? You are allowed to get assistance in areas that make you uncomfortable. Balance is about being okay with not being perfect.

In addition, be open to saying yes. If there is a new way or opportunity to improve your caregiving experience, you can try saying yes instead of staying with strategies or ways of doing things that feel easy because they are familiar. When you are open to saying yes to people who offer to help you, who are willing to step in when they see you struggling, or who offer a supportive suggestion, you are moving toward more balance. Saying yes allows you the space and energy to get back on track with a fresh outlook.

You can't always ride right down the middle of the road, nor can you always be as balanced as you wish. Accepting that everyone gets thrown off balance and being kind to yourself about it is the first step to getting that balance back. Forgiveness, self-awareness, and saying yes will guide you.

Stay In Touch with Your Spirituality

Caregiving can stretch the limits of the emotional and spiritual reserves of even the heartiest of people. Having faith in a higher power not only helps in day-to-day life; it can make the unbearable bearable and the impossible possible.

Don't get too busy or too discouraged to stay in touch with the higher power of your choice. Keeping the faith is a nonnegotiable, must-have strategy in the caregiver's arsenal. Without faith in something, you can feel clueless and lost. With it, you can be a centered, peaceful caregiver, powering on even when your day feels awful, endless, and futile.

If celebrating your faith at a specific time or on a specific day feels right to you, do your best to continue this ritual. With today's technology, livestreaming or recorded events are easy to find, so you can feel the comfort of your faith even if you can't leave the house.

If meditation or being in nature or listening to music are your connections to a higher power, participate in these activities as often as you can for relief and solace. Don't wait until you are literally on your knees in caregiver despair before you are in touch with your faith to soothe your soul.

Most importantly, don't forget you can be mad at your higher power and still have faith. Caregivers have many burdens to bear that can cause frustration and pain, and letting loose with anger and confusion is understandable. Your higher power will understand.

Listen to Your Heart

Caregivers are often creative thinkers. Confronted with all sorts of dilemmas that require a lot of thought while navigating the world of caregiving, many caregivers rely on analyzing the problems to find the answer. Making the best decisions for those they care for can begin to look and feel like a puzzle. Caregiving relies on logical, rational thinking, but ruminating about and going over and over a problem can make it worse. Negative thoughts and ruminating are upsetting and distracting, and can cause anxiety.

It may well be time you begin to listen to your heart instead of the noisy conversations going on in your head that never seem to get you anywhere. Listening to your heart or your intuition means tuning in to your emotions and feelings rather than your intellect.

Getting quiet with meditation is helpful because it quiets the mind and helps get you in touch with what you are feeling, not what you are thinking. Taking a five-minute break from caregiving to sit quietly and concentrate on your body and soul instead of the chatter in your head can clarify the true issue.

While sitting quietly, ask yourself how each of the possible options or solutions you believe you have makes you feel. Which options make you feel calm and relieved? Which ones just don't feel right? You will "know" what feels better. Trusting this intuitive feeling is exactly what caregivers need to do when the mind can't come up with an answer. Your heart will tell you.

Communicate with the Family

When you are taking care of family members, it can be an extremely complicated process, and usually everyone in the family is involved in one way or another. There is usually one person who steps up as the primary caregiver. This decision can be based on geographical proximity, but it is often due to one person feeling the need or desire to take on the responsibility.

It may be hard to keep the rest of the family in the loop, especially if any of the relationships are rocky, or if family members don't get along or have opposing opinions about the care the loved one should be getting. This can be especially stressful for the primary caregiver.

Communication is a master tool that can be used to alleviate this tension within the family. If everyone is always in the loop and communicating, it's easier to stay on the same page and avoid disagreements or bad feelings. Even when the family supports you and all that you do, being open and communicative can offer them peace of mind during the caregiving journey because they feel a part of it all. Feeling involved can be the balm that heals the family.

How you choose to communicate is a personal choice and depends on your family situation and the methods they prefer. You should be a consistent and constant communicator. This will inspire support, new perspectives, and help, and can prevent arguments. Family members may be upset and frustrated with the fact that someone they love has changed and is declining or suffering, and they may feel they are not doing enough to help. If they are kept aware of all that is happening and have the opportunity to ask questions, be updated, and share their feelings, you can defuse their anger and frustration and commiserate with them about your fear and sadness. They might surprise you with a great suggestion you hadn't thought of.

Remember to include those you care for in the mix if they are able to participate in family discussions and communications. Making decisions as a family is always a smart, constructive idea, and inclusive communication allows this to happen in a positive, healthy way.

Set up a weekly or daily Zoom meeting, phone call, or in-person discussion when possible and make sure it happens, but also make sure it happens at a time that is good for you. Delegate the organizing of it to someone else so you can just be a participant. Tell the family you are always happy to be in touch and to check in at other times, but it's important to have a scheduled time when everyone can come together.

Create a group text so you can always send an update or a family member can reach you with questions or support and continue the conversation. Make boundaries about the times you will be available and remind everyone of those times if necessary.

Be honest and open and willing to listen. Ask everyone to do the same. Effective communication creates a supportive, empathetic, and understanding family caregiving experience.

Set Boundaries

Caregivers are often great multitaskers, yet even when they don't have a moment to spare they still might be called on to add more duties or commitments to an already overbooked schedule. When this happens, it's time to set boundaries and learn to say no.

Setting boundaries begins with being aware that you might be taking on too much because you want to please or take care of everyone. Caregivers are usually good-natured about trying to help out. Yet, when your stress level or schedule starts to become overwhelming, it's time to start honoring yourself and pick and choose what you can and cannot do and then share this information with everyone.

Look closely at a typical day in your caregiving life. To do this, write down and keep track of everything you do and accomplish in a day. This should give you a good snapshot of how much gets done. Add to it things you wish you had time to take care of if you had more hours in the day.

If you are like most caregivers, you are going to be surprised by the number of activities and goals that were reached in this one day. Yet even with all that you have accomplished, there are still the pressing things you would add if you had more time.

Now see if there is space for one more added request from someone else in your day. It probably feels impossible and upsetting to add anything to your already jam-packed day. The point of this exercise is to see that you have a legitimate reason to feel pressure when asked to do something that you don't have the time or energy to do. There's no reason to feel bad or guilty!

When you are asked to do something that will be too much for you or something you don't want to do, it's time to say, "I'm sorry. I'm unable to do that." Most people will understand, and those that don't do not have your best interests at heart. Be patient but firm with them. You can always show them the list you made of your daily caregiving life.

"No" is a complete sentence. You don't have to overexplain why you are unable to do something. If you want to, a brief, honest explanation can help others begin to understand how busy and complicated a caregiver's life can be. This might help them be more sensitive in the future, but remember you are always entitled to politely say no with or without an explanation.

Boundaries are a caregiver's best friend. It may feel awkward at first to say no, or that you can't do something, but the more you honor yourself, your time, and your energy, the easier it will become to set healthy boundaries. You know best when something will be too much for you—be firm and confident about it.

Learn When to Lean In or Back Off

Caregiving is all about balance. Staying centered and in the middle of the road as much as you can is always the goal. This balance helps you be your best self and navigate the caregiving world. This balance also helps you know when to lean in and when to back off.

Being tenacious when attempting to reach a goal is an important skill, as is the ability to know when to back off and let things go. The balance between these two skills takes finesse and experience. Knowing when to lean in and keep going or when to ease up and let go takes some getting used to. Ask yourself the following questions and use the answer to guide you about whether you should keep pushing at something or let go of it. Your body, mind, and intuition can help guide you to which tactic would be best to use.

> How do you feel right now? Are you frustrated and angry, or are you in a positive, hopeful space?

If you feel angry and under tons of pressure, you might be trying to force a solution. It might be best to put off what you are doing or stop pushing so hard to make it go your way. Try letting go and backing off. Letting go and letting the universe catch up to all the hard work you are doing allows you to get a new perspective and come up with different tactics when you return to it later.

If you feel centered and hopeful that you can get what you need and achieve the outcome you desire, keep at it. Don't get discouraged or take things personally. Many situations and circumstances in the caregiving world take numerous attempts to reach goals. Visualize the outcome in your mind and keep trying.

Say for instance you are dealing with your loved one's health insurance to get preapproved for an important medical test that will be astronomically expensive if you don't have the preapproval. If you are calm and relaxed and surrender to the fact that you might have to be on hold for a long time, checking and double-checking that the preapproval did indeed go through, you will be better able to stay with it until you get what you need. If the representative has a difficult personality and you feel like you're not getting anywhere, excuse yourself and say you have to take another call, then hang up, call back, and speak to someone else.

If no matter what you do you can't get someone to help you or you are hitting a wall and pulling your hair out and getting rude or impatient, it's time to let it go, take a break, and move on to something else.

The more you get in touch with your feelings around issues you are pushing for, the better you will be at knowing when to keep going and when to let go.

Say What You Mean, Mean What You Say, but Don't Say It Mean

Communication is a critical aspect of caregiving. What you say and how you say it influences and determines every experience you have. Each caregiving situation is different, but during difficult conversations, this phrase can bring you outstanding results: "Say what you mean, mean what you say, but don't say it mean."

Remember this saying when you are trying to have effective and empathetic conversations with those you care for, your team and family, and those who help you care for your loved ones.

- **Say what you mean.** You need to be honest and authentic. Stop and think before you address an issue, make a point, or give feedback. What do you want to say? Choose your words carefully because they have great power. Words not based on truth, kindness, and empathy do nothing more than hurt feelings and close down communication. Saying what you mean can help to establish a great rapport or create a lousy one. Caregiving is all about relationships and how you nurture them.
- **Mean what you say.** To be effective and clear as a caregiver, there's no beating around the bush. Be committed to what you are saying without using innuendos or trying to avoid feelings. Be as fearless in your everyday conversation as you are as a caregiver. Don't be afraid to be yourself, even if it means being vulnerable or having tough conversations.
- **Don't say it mean.** Most importantly, no matter what you say, don't say it in a mean way. Sarcasm, accusatory language, and condescension are guaranteed to alienate people and get you into hot water because they may trigger all sorts of negative responses. Being nasty is childish and senseless. Pay attention to how you sound. If you hear yourself sounding snarky, stop it immediately and ask yourself what's going on with you. What feelings are

causing you to take your frustration out on someone else? That needs to be resolved on your time.

Also, be aware of your tone of voice. Your tone communicates your actual feelings, regardless of the words you use. When caring for patients with dementia, Alzheimer's, or cognitive decline, there will be times that they will not understand the words you say but they will clearly understand by your tone whether you are being kind and understanding or frustrated and annoyed.

Try experimenting with this. Pause before speaking and see if you can start a conversation with kindness and an authentic, gentle, loving tone of voice. Pay close attention to the response you get, especially with those you serve. You might even see a softening of their body or face. What seems to be such a small gesture on your part can have a huge impact. Remembering this saying and applying it to every conversation you have can make a major shift in your caregiving world.

Ask for Help

Most caregivers find it hard to ask for help. For some reason, they think there is some unwritten law that says if you reach out and ask for help you have failed as a caregiver. Or they believe that no one else can take care of their loved ones the way they do. The truth is, caregiving takes a village, and there isn't a caregiver in the world that can do it alone indefinitely. The cost on their body, mind, and soul is too great and, eventually, they will break down and then be unable to do the job that means so much to them.

Consider these thoughts and take the following actions when you feel like you are sinking and realize you need help but feel too ashamed, embarrassed, or worried about no one doing the job the way you can.

- **Accept help!** There are people all around you in your tribe and family and friends that watch you and what you are going through and want to help. Most of them don't know what to say, what to do, or how to help. At some point, they will offer to lend a hand. Even if it's not something you necessarily need help with, say yes anyway! This gets the ball rolling, letting them know you are open to their assistance and encouraging them to offer help in other ways. You can always be honest and tell them that you are struggling in another area and ask if they would consider pitching in with that.
- **Start with little things.** To make it easier to get used to asking for help, start small. Instead of leaving your loved ones with someone else for the day, ask them to sit and visit with them for an hour while you are still in the house doing other things to see how it goes. Perhaps you can ask someone to accompany you to the doctor's office to show them the ropes so they could drive your loved one the next time. Give them a small grocery list if they offer to shop for you. You can slowly build up to having helpers in

your life, especially when you begin to see how good it feels and how much it helps with your workload.

- **Change the way you look at things.** Try seeing things from the point of view of those who want to help. If your best friend or sister or brother were struggling, you would be the first to jump in to help them. The shoe is simply on the other foot. Let those who love you step in as you would for them, as you have for those you care for.

Asking for help isn't about being weak or incompetent; it *is* about being brave and realistic. It may be true that no one will do things exactly the way you do, but when others lend a hand after you ask for help, you are getting a much-needed break that will allow you to regroup and recharge. There is no downside to that.

Let Empathy Guide You

Of all the caregiver self-help tools, empathy might just yield the most enduring and powerful results of all. Being empathetic means that you have the ability to understand and share the feelings of others, from their point of view, placing yourself in their situation.

This is priceless in terms of helping you be kind, patient, and understanding. It allows you to see the message under the words or behavior and gives you the ability to stay objective and loving. Use empathy to guide you in your caregiving journey. Tap in to the healing it offers, even during times of exhaustion when you have little left to give.

Take some time to think about your loved one and what they are feeling physically and emotionally. Imagine being in their shoes and experiencing the life changes they are going through and how that might affect them. If it were you, how might it make you feel and how would you act? Can you empathize with how scared, confused, and frustrated they might be?

When communicating with them, connect with them. Sit and listen and instead of trying to fix them, tell them you understand and appreciate what they are going through. Treat them with respect. Quite often they just want to be heard and acknowledged. When you are empathetic, they can feel it. They feel validated and loved. Empathy creates kinship so love and healing can be shared. Let it guide you to a deeper, more connected relationship with those you lovingly care for.

Chapter 4: Practical Self-Care

Caregiving has a huge practical aspect to it. Planning, organizing, scheduling, details, and medical and health protocols are just the tip of the iceberg. Add to that team management, relationship building and maintenance, and legal and financial administration—all of which take an enormous amount of time and energy. This is in addition to being attentive to the physical and emotional needs of patients with a wide variety of symptoms and medical conditions.

Managing all the details of caregiving takes persistence, perseverance, patience, and enormous effort, so having powerful strategies to lean on is imperative. Knowing whom to call, when to call, and how to manage the call takes finesse. While most caregivers possess these qualities to begin with, there are techniques and actions that can enhance and improve your ability to get things done more efficiently and with less strain.

Taking the stress and worry out of the logistics of caregiving is what this chapter is about. Here you will find practical tips, actions, and activities that help you get organized, be prepared for anything, and successfully navigate the caregiving obstacle course.

Information is power and organization is lifesaving. These practical self-care directives give you all the information and organizational tools you need to handle the day-to-day details of how to keep the caregiving machine running smoothly. When added to your caregiver arsenal they can help you develop a plan of action that gets you from overwhelmed to in command.

Track Your Time

Keeping track of your time is a powerful way to stay organized and focused. Once you try it and make it a habit, you might be shocked at how impactful it can be on your caregiving duties. You will find that certain tasks take longer than you think, which allows you to plan accordingly and avoid stress, and you might find some extra time you can take for yourself. Time tracking shows you exactly how you spend your time so you can manage it, stop wasting it, and use it more effectively.

Try using the clock app on your phone to time your activities or set alarms for specific times. For example, give yourself an hour to do phone calls or work on your loved one's finances. When the timer goes off, take a five-minute break. Jot down how much you got done. Do this for a week to see if you become more efficient.

Another way to keep track is to write down what you are doing and how long it takes you. Keep a notebook nearby and jot down activities, tasks, and actions. Keep track for a week and see your pattern. Do not forget to add in breaks, relaxation, and downtime! Time those activities too.

Take a good look at what you accomplish, how long it takes you, and if you get distracted or waste time. Once you are aware of how you spend your time, you can manage it so it works for you.

Pause Between Reaction and Action

Caregivers are action takers. Keeping up with the whirlwind responsibilities of caregiving is possible only if you move decisively and quickly. However, there is a tiny but significant trick to getting the most out of what happens to you and how you respond to it. When you have to handle something like unexpected changes in your loved one's condition or their refusal to eat or take medication, you should pause between your reaction and the action you take. While it's true that you need to be proactive and respond accordingly, taking a moment to pause can serve you.

Instead of rushing in to save the day, you should pause, reflect, and feel. It takes effort and practice, but it also only takes a minute. Before moving forward, reflect on what's going on and how it's affecting everyone, then see how it makes you feel. This is a great time to see what your "gut" is telling you. That quiet voice has great wisdom. Do you need to be extra gentle with those you care for, do you need to take a break, is this an emergency? What are the options and their consequences? Once you have taken this pause, reflection, and emotional check-in, you will be clearer on the next right move, and rather than acting on impulse you can act on reason and intuition. This tiny pause has a world of possibility in it.

Be Willing to Learn

One of the greatest gifts of caregiving is all the things you learn along the way. You learn about those you love and care for and you learn about yourself. Caregiving is an extraordinary experience, and if you lean in to it, as hard as it is, it can open your eyes and heart like nothing else. For this reason, you must always find a way to be willing to stay curious and be open to the wealth of wisdom you can gain. You must work at this willingness since there will be days when you feel as though your brain cannot take one more new piece of information. It's easy to feel that your hard drive is full and your learning capacity has been met. Yet curiosity and a thirst for knowledge can change the caregiving role from tedious to engaging.

Try these tips and see if they help to remind you to stay open and curious.

- **Don't be afraid to try new things.** It may feel easier to stick to what seems to work and is familiar. Stepping out of your comfort zone might feel like a stretch, but mixing it up and trying something new has two benefits. The first is that it builds confidence and self-worth. The second is that the new perspective almost always improves your life.
- **Check in with other caregivers.** Chat with another caregiver and find out how they do things. Especially something you find difficult, boring, or distasteful. Hearing a new take on things can be eye-opening. Even the most mundane task can be more interesting if you learn a different way to do it.
- **Don't lose your desire for knowledge.** Don't get stuck in a rut. Although it feels safer to keep plowing through the day doing the same old same old, having something new to look forward to is stimulating and motivating.
- **Try learning one small new thing a day.** Pick one small thing you can learn about each day. It can be anything from a word or a song, to a new

joke to tell your loved one or a new recipe, even a new drug side effect! It doesn't have to be something that changes the world; it just must make one small change for you.

- **Seek out some stories you've never heard before from those you care for.** Ask your loved ones about happy or favorite times in their lives. If they can't remember or communicate, ask their peers or other family members or friends to tell you a story they love about the person. A whole new world of information is waiting for discovery.

Learning new things, shaking it up, and giving yourself a small challenge helps break up the tedium and gets you reenergized. Even the most experienced caregiver can stretch and learn and reap the benefits of new, useful, and even fun information.

Research Drug Interactions and Side Effects

It's important to stay on top of the medications your loved one is taking. Since multiple doctors may be prescribing different medications, it's always possible that a drug one doctor prescribed could interfere with a drug prescribed by another doctor. Drug interactions can be tricky, and you need to be knowledgeable and aware of these possible interactions.

As well as the drug interactions, possible side effects of any drugs should also be discussed and researched. It saves so much heartache to know what to expect, how long side effects last, and what is cause for alarm.

When new drugs are being offered, ask questions. Have your up-to-date, current medication list with you so you can discuss what is already prescribed and the compatibility of all the drugs. Let the doctor know you want to make sure all the medications are safe and work together. Go over the possible side effects with the doctor.

Check with your pharmacist too, and ask if they suggest any special administering instructions and if they are aware of any interactions that you need to make note of. Having the doctor and pharmacist on the same page makes mistakes avoidable.

Also, when possible, be sure to include the patient that will be taking the drugs in the discussion so they clearly understand the benefits and risks and can participate in any decision, if they are able to do so. When you have all the information you need and everyone involved working together, medications can enhance the quality of life as intended.

Get the Donkey Out of the Ditch

Much of caregiver self-care has to do with managing time, stealing time, watching time, and making time. The last thing caregivers want or need to do is waste time. After all, they never have enough of it to begin with.

So if your proverbial donkey ends up in a ditch, you can't waste time wondering how it got there; you need to focus on how to get it out. Worrying or fretting about the situation doesn't get you any closer to solving it. Trying to speculate or ruminate about what happened and why distracts you from problem-solving.

So do this instead. Get out of the problem and into the solution. Stop worrying about why and how you got here. It doesn't matter now. If you are responsible for the problem you are now facing, admit and accept that and pledge to do better. Learn from it, gracefully and gratefully take any lesson it has taught you, and make sure to use this useful information later.

Now start thinking about how to fix it. Picture what you want to happen and start to come up with ways to get you there. Start planning and devising the solution. Your brain is an amazing computer system, and once you ask it to fix a problem, it goes to town. Put it to work by seeking an answer to the puzzle in front of you, and, before you know it, the donkey is out of the ditch, and you are both on your way.

Work Smarter, Not Harder

The faster you can cut to the chase and get things accomplished, the easier it is to manage all the moving parts of caregiving. You must be flexible and get into a working rhythm that allows you to keep things humming.

This rhythm has nothing to do with working harder or working longer hours. It has everything to do with working smarter. When you work smarter, you are more efficient with your time and energy. Try the following suggestions to see if they help you work smarter.

- **Set up goals for the next day.** Setting up your goals the night before gives you a jump start on your day when you wake up. Come up with a list of things you can do to reach your goal, listing the most important and daunting tasks first. Your brain will work on it during the night and have answers in the morning. You can even come up with a general list of goals if you are too exhausted to devise plans. The point of the exercise is to think about tomorrow's possibilities and then sleep on them!

- **Do one thing at a time.** Trying to juggle six things at once is confusing, time-wasting, and stressful. You can get discombobulated by letting your attention be pulled in too many directions at once. Take a small bite and concentrate on eating that one bite. The whole sandwich gets eaten one bite at a time.

- **Do the hardest thing first.** Get the biggest, scariest thing out of the way first. Do it the first thing when you have the most energy. The rest will feel so much easier, and the pressure will be off. If you jump into the cold water all at once, you can get used to it more quickly and then begin to enjoy it. By doing the hardest stuff first, you no longer have it hanging over your head or worrying you. Now you can relax and do the easier things.

- **Get rid of distractions.** Lose social media, TV, news, messy desks, tables, environments, and even people. Give yourself a clear working space, with as much quiet as possible, and do everything you can to promote a positive working environment and vibe.

- **Take breaks!** You have only so much attention and energy, and the best way to work smarter is to take breaks. When you begin to feel distracted or your mind and body feel tired, stop what you are doing and walk away from it. You'll return refreshed and have more to offer.

Keep Up with the Spinning Plates

The spinning plates of caregiving and how you keep them spinning is no joke. It takes more than magic to keep your plates spinning day after day. It takes focus, energy, and determination. You need to move from plate to plate with ease and balance. Here are some practical tips to keep those plates from falling and breaking into pieces around you.

First, focus on one plate at a time. Pay attention to whatever is about to go off-kilter and crash. That's the most important one to concentrate on. Do what it takes to stabilize the situation and get it "spinning" in a smooth, balanced way. Put all your weight behind adjusting or correcting the situation. Trust that the other things that need your attention will be fine while you tackle this one. Once you've got that issue on its way to being resolved, you can move on to the next plate and forget about the last one. Put your complete focus on the new spinning plate that needs your adjustment.

Moving back and forth between spinning issues takes dexterity and concentration. Everything keeps moving if you take one plate at a time, adjust, then let it go and jump to the next. There is a rhythm and a flow, and although it will take practice, you will learn to juggle and spin by staying fluid and focused.

Keep an Updated Contact List

Once you have your caregiving team in place, it's vital to keep track of them. Compile a detailed contact list that includes names, contact info, and designated roles, and keep it where it can be easily accessed. Even though you may have their phone numbers memorized or on speed dial, it's wise to remember that should something happen to you, whoever is designated to step in will need to access these numbers quickly. Always keep the list with you and distribute it to the team. Rather than taking for granted that everyone knows how to contact each other, or that you will always be the contact point, update this list and distribute it as soon as changes are made.

Writing down the services and help others are willing and able to give and how often next to each person's name is also extremely helpful. In case of an emergency, the names of those who can show up quickly and are willing and able should be highlighted. This is invaluable if someone new needs to step in or you need immediate help but are overwhelmed and have to pinpoint someone quickly. This list can be in the order of the most available, or the legal next of kin, or any order that works best for you. It's a great idea to include the police department, fire department, doctors, hospitals, family members, and legal representations. This way anyone involved can jump in without fumbling in case of emergency. This is your team, keep their information close by.

Manage Meds Effectively

How you manage and administer medication is an integral part of caregiving, but sometimes this task can make even the most seasoned caregiver crazy. At some point in your caregiving experience, you will likely have a mind-boggling amount of pills and potions to administer.

When are medications given, how many are given, is it half a pill or whole, should they be taken with food, without food, do they interact with each other, and, of course, what do you do if they are missed or forgotten? These are just a few of the things you need to worry about. The mountain of pills seems to grow with time, but don't let it engulf you! Make medications work for you, not against you, by using the following tactics.

- Get a few large plastic pill holders with a.m. and p.m. slots for seven days and fill them up for a week or even two weeks. This can save an enormous amount of time because it's a task that is done once a week instead of daily.
- Spreadsheets and large printed schedules of the medications with the day and time they are administered with dosages, descriptions, and the prescribing doctor are helpful tools. Keep them on the refrigerator and/or by the pill containers. Anyone can refer to them if need be.
- Keeping a list of the medications with you at all times on your phone or a flash drive or printed out is critical. You never know when you will need to refer to it or hand it over to healthcare professionals. Thinking you can commit it to memory especially under duress in an emergency is not practical. Update this list as soon as it changes and give the updated list to anyone who holds a copy of it.
- Make sure every doctor and every nurse on every shift has the list. Have an easily accessible copy to offer them to check or keep. And when there is a change of ward or floor or facility, go over the list with head nurses and

attending physicians. Confirm that anyone and everyone administering the medications has the most current list.

- Never assume that doctors, nurses, or aides have all the information they need, especially when it comes to medications. Err on the side of caution by going over the medications again and again. You are entitled to ask questions and reassure yourself that everyone is aware of the medications on the list. Know what to expect when a new medication is prescribed and how it works.

Managing medications is a full-time job. Keeping a complete, updated list handy and giving it to the people who need to see it is critical. Drugs are amazing tools that can save lives, but they are dangerous if not taken seriously and managed with care. Keep everyone on the same page so these wonder drugs can do their magic safely.

Don't Assume

When you assume anything, you are asking for disaster. This is true for life in general but is extremely true in the caregiving world. You can't take anything for granted or assume you know what is happening, what might be happening, or what's about to happen. When you assume you understand things without knowledge or proof, you are opening yourself up to trouble. Here are three "assume" traps to avoid.

- **Do not assume you can handle your caregiving role alone.** It cannot and will not work. You are headed for caregiver burnout. All caregivers assume this from time to time but soon get over it and reach out for help.
- **Don't assume you understand what your loved ones are capable of.** Their condition changes from day to day, and it's important not to expect too much today because they were able and strong yesterday or to underestimate what they can do tomorrow because today is a bad day. Make sure to evaluate their condition daily.
- **Lastly, don't assume your loved one doesn't understand you.** Just because you don't get a positive response or, sometimes, any response at all, it doesn't mean they don't understand. Compliance and sometimes silence can be misleading. Giving everyone the benefit of the doubt and believing they understand you is courteous and respectful; it creates the possibility that your loved ones will surprise you and respond!

Put One Foot in Front of the Other

A caregiver's path unfolds one step at a time. If you forget that and look at the big picture too often or out of context, it can be frightening. So staying present in the moment and putting one foot in front of the other helps to keep you grounded and makes it all feel doable. When you drill down into the smaller parts of the whole, you begin to go to work.

This metaphor of putting one foot in front of the other can help you see that if you want to climb a mountain, you will never do it by standing at the bottom looking up at it. You only reach the top by starting the climb, and you start the climb by taking the first step and then another.

You travel through your caregiving experience by making one good choice at a time, not only for your loved ones but for yourself. Choices are flying at you from all directions, but if you deliberately deal with one choice at a time, you are going in a good, orderly direction. Before you know it, you have created change and resolved problems.

Slow down your racing mind by pausing, breathing, and focusing on one thing. Resolve that issue and pat yourself on the back for taking that step. Repeat, breathe, pause, and focus on the next action and make the next right choice. Putting one choice, one foot in front of the other gets you moving up the mountain and over the top.

Get the Most Out of Doctors' Visits

Wouldn't it be nice if caregivers got frequent flyer miles from doctors? You could end up with free examinations for yourself and those you love! Since this doesn't exist, you can at least make the doctors' visits you go to as efficient, effective, and pleasant as possible.

- **Be nice.** Make everyone you meet in the doctor's office your new best friend. Be pleasant, conversational, and patient. Everyone, especially frazzled nurses, appreciates nice, kind people. The treatment you get reflects the treatment you give. Remember, you might be seeing these people often!
- **Prepare early for a doctor's visit.** Of course, you never want those you care for to wait longer than they have to in a waiting room, but allowing enough time at home for dressing, resistance, or small problems helps to keep everyone calm and not feel rushed. Build in plenty of extra time for this.
- **Make a list of questions.** Write down everything you want and need to ask. Be confident and assertive when you make this list. If something concerns you, write it down. You are paying for the doctor's time, so take advantage of it. Tell the doctor you have a list of questions, and when they are finished with the examination you want to read it to them. This prepares them and establishes what you need. It also lets them concentrate and focus on the examination without having to be distracted by questions.
- **Make a list of symptoms.** Have every symptom and any new developments written down so you can read them to the doctor. It's easy to forget something in the heat of the moment. It's best to review these symptoms or update the doctor at the beginning of the visit so they know what to look for.

- **Bring the medication list.** Have that trusty list of current medications available during the post-examination discussion. If new medications are being prescribed, you can refer to it and make sure everyone is on the same page and the doctor is aware of current medications. It will save the doctor time and avoid negative interactions.

- **Record the post-examination discussion.** If everyone is comfortable, you could record the conversation on your phone. If this doesn't feel appropriate, you can always take notes. Just let the doctor know you want to make sure you remember everything. People tend to forget things when they are on edge or stressed.

- **Include those you care for.** If your loved one is capable of participating in the interaction with the doctor, include them and let them be involved. Work with them to create the questions and symptoms lists. If you are the point of contact during the visit, include them in the list-making anyway. This will allow them to feel heard, respected, and consulted about their health and well-being.

Following these guidelines will make those doctors' visits less stressful, and you'll get more bang for your buck!

Keep a "Go Bag" of Essentials by the Front Door

Keep a bag of important, necessary items handy, always. If you can conveniently place it by the front door so you just grab it on the go, even better. It's best to put it somewhere that you can't miss or forget it if you are rushing around in an emergency or unexpectedly taking someone to the hospital or emergency room.

Here are some good suggestions for items you will be happy you packed in that bag.

- Sweatshirts or light sweaters are great when you find yourself in waiting and ER rooms. Most healthcare institutions keep the temperature very cool to minimize germ growth, so having the comfort of an extra layer is always welcome.
- Keep a few printed lists of the updated, current medications for the patient with your contact information on them. Although it's always good to verbally check off the medications with the administering staff, a written backup is valuable. And if you change departments or have new staff arrive as shifts change, you can always hand this over and have them check it against what was transferred to them by the previous staff.
- Bring phone chargers. The last thing you need is your phone to run out of battery. Take a charger for you and your loved ones. There's always an outlet!
- Include some healthy snacks. Pack your favorite healthy energy bar for you and favorite snacks for your loved ones. Throwing in a few bottles of water or sweeteners such as stevia can't hurt either.
- Add in magazines and that paperback you've been meaning to get to. Make sure the magazines are fun and interesting to everyone that's with you.
- Tissues, hand sanitizer, and wipes are indispensable. These are must-haves anywhere you go.

- Finally, include any legal documents such as healthcare proxy, medical wishes, medical and financial powers of attorney, and any other designated guardian paperwork. You should have a copy of all of these on your phone if possible, but hard copies can be required in certain instances and are always great to hand over to administration.

Add anything you feel would make you and those you care for safe, more comfortable, less stressed, and entertained. Having this "go bag" ready to grab and go is the ultimate preplanning. The last thing you want to do is run around trying to find all the things you might need in an emergency room or doctor's office when you are in a rush or not thinking clearly because you are in crisis mode. Providing yourself with this easy solution is great self-care for you and also so considerate of those in your care.

Do One Task at a Time

A caregiver's work is never done. It can feel like you are racing against a clock that keeps changing. New developments arise every day, sometimes every hour, and there is always so much that needs to be done. Even the most prepared and experienced caregivers scramble to keep up with the changes they are presented with constantly. Sometimes it feels like the more you take care of, the faster the challenges come.

You need to focus on the task at hand, one task at a time. Knocking off one thing at a time as opposed to multitasking is the only way to clear a path through the jungle. Here's where your prioritized lists come in handy, helping you to spotlight the task right in front of you. Even the most disciplined caregiver can get sidetracked by feeling overwhelmed by multiple tasks waiting in the wings. When this happens, gently bring your attention back to what you are doing right here, right now, and finish the task at hand. Stay in the present, reengage with what you are doing, and ignore any nagging worry about the future. You might have to do this refocusing several times, but once you can stay present and engaged, you'll start to fly through that to-do list one task at a time.

Keep Moving

There will be times during your caregiving day when you will feel tired, discouraged, and disgruntled. You might feel frozen and stuck in the mud with no inspiration. It's hard at times like these to find a reason to keep going, even when you know you have to.

Take off the superhero cape and instead of trying to *do*, just *be*. Just show up. Don't wait for motivation, since motivation rarely arrives, just try to relax and continue to go through the motions without doing it perfectly.

It's when you just show up and keep moving, no matter how much resistance you feel, that you are sometimes able to do your best work. You don't have to have the answers or solutions. Sometimes you need to take your goals and throw them out the window because you are tired. Letting go of the pressure you put on yourself to be a cheerful, caregiving machine can be just what you need.

Pick the easiest task or the simplest action and do it or take it. Make an appearance. Do the minimum, but do something. You don't have to win any awards. You just need to be present and involved. The rest will fall into place; one action leads to another, you build momentum, and things start to break loose. Just keep things in motion, and you will get there before you know it.

Create Effective To-Do Lists

Making a to-do list sounds like one of the easiest and most logical things a caregiver can do. Why, then, do so many of us put it off?

The sheer number of things that need to be done may be the culprit. However, the list is so much bigger in your head than on a piece of paper. The fastest way to defeat the fear around your to-dos is to write them down. They are never as daunting on the page in front of you as they are in your mind.

Try making your list first thing in the morning—think of it as a road map for the day. Ask yourself what your intention is and what you can write down that will help you have a good day. Make it a practical list of things you want to accomplish, making sure to add things you'd like to do for yourself.

For every three practical tasks, write down one self-care assignment. Try to write your list with a feeling of possibility instead of a feeling of dread. To-do lists can carry a feeling of avoidance around them if you approach them with panic and defeat. However, if you approach them as tools with the potential to help you organize and accomplish, they become positive starting points.

Now look over the list a few times and pick three of the most important and helpful tasks and one doable self-care assignment and put them in a separate list. That's the list you work on first! As you knock off the items on this first list, you can re-visit your original morning list if you have the time or energy to begin the process again, or if you have reached the end of your day, celebrate what you accomplished. Tomorrow will offer another chance to conquer another to-do list!

Take the Action, Then Let Go of the Results

The caregiving job description reads like that of the head of a major corporation: take-charge ability, self-motivated, can-do attitude, able to take on large important projects and meet goals in a timely fashion.

Most caregivers, however, in their desire to do so much and do it effectively, can get caught up in the results of their actions rather than just accomplishing them. Seeing the end game is always helpful, but getting caught up in things going your way, or the way you want them to go, can set up expectations that won't be met. Making a commitment to doing the next right thing, regardless of how perfectly it will turn out, offers you a reprieve from the need to be perfect.

Once you take the action, let go of the results. If you have thought it through, weighed the pros and cons, and have everyone's best interest at heart, trust that the perfect solution will emerge, and that you have done all you can for now. No matter what the outcome is, you have met the challenge head-on with good intention and did your best to resolve it. You've done all the hard work, now let the universe catch up to you and take care of the rest. Move on to the next action. Celebrate your ability to get things done, regardless of the outcome.

Just Move the Needle

Let's face it, when you are caring for someone's else health and well-being, the stakes are high. Caregivers can feel an enormous amount of pressure to make major improvements or positive changes as quickly as possible in the lives of those they care for. So the results seem like they need to be dramatic or exceptional. At certain times, this indeed needs to happen, but usually there is something to be said about steady, small results and the important role they can play.

Caregivers don't always give themselves enough credit for moving the needle a little at a time. They underestimate the significance and importance of making even the smallest changes to things that are affecting their loved ones. Often, disaster can be avoided by this steady change in the right direction, even if it's a little bit at a time.

Recognize the little wins. If you have made a strategic move in the right direction, give yourself lots of credit. Appreciate the initiative and consistency. Review your overall plan and recognize that not only are you going in the right direction; you are also making a big difference. Everything doesn't have to be dramatic or instantaneous or life-changing.

Moving the needle a little at a time and achieving small wins adds up, and suddenly a major shift happens. Don't wait until all the dominos fall to feel proud, confident, and capable. You are getting closer to the goal and the plan is working.

Deal With Distraction

Even though caregiving requires extreme concentration, even the best of us can become distracted when in the middle of a caregiving chore. Here are a few self-care tricks to help you stay on point.

- **Be aware.** Be conscious of how you are spending your time. Are you yawning, are you thinking about a million other things, are you looking around, do you feel tired? Your attention is slipping away. Make a note and do something about it.
- **Take a break.** You need a break. Do something that isn't about caregiving. It's pointless to keep on with what you are doing. Come back to it refreshed after a mini-break. Now would be a great time for a quick snack or a stretch or ten minutes of meditation. You can always time the break if it makes you feel less guilty.
- **Move on to something else.** If you don't want to take a break, pick up another chore instead of what you are doing so you can feel refreshed or challenged by a new activity. When you switch things up it's like a brain restart. You can go back to the other chore later and finish it faster.

Being kind to yourself when you get distracted is so much better than trying to force yourself to keep going. Acknowledging that you need to do something else or take a break saves so much time and energy in the long run.

Schedule Like a Pro

Making and sticking to a schedule is a terrific way to reduce caregiver burnout and worry. Schedules help you prioritize and stay organized so you withstand the chaos that caregiving can cause. Whether these schedules are kept on your phone, on a large wall calendar that everyone can refer to, or in a book you can glance at, schedules keep the caregiving train puffing along.

Follow these helpful hints to make a schedule you can rely on and work with if the ground shifts under your feet. How you use and view your schedules can make all the difference in your caregiving world.

- **Prioritize.** Be realistic and practical about how much can get done in a day. Pick the most pressing things and add them to your schedule first. Less is best. Under-promise and over-deliver. If you cram in too much, it only gives you a reason to freak out when you can't possibly get it all done. It's even wise to schedule only a few things to begin with. If you end up having extra time left over, you can always add something in. That's so much better than having to take things out!
- **Be mindful of the energy around what you schedule.** When scheduling, give yourself room between important appointments that are upsetting or traumatizing to you or your loved ones. Keep your schedule clearer on those days so you all have time to recuperate. Be mindful of what you schedule and where.
- **Always leave plenty of room for the expected unexpected.** On top of being realistic and putting a little less activity in the schedule, it's a good idea to compensate for the extra time needed around the tasks you do put on the schedule. Build in lots of time for things like the unexpected resistance from your loved ones and the all-too-often last-minute snags and wrench-in-the-works propositions. As all caregivers are aware, even when things go smoothly, they never go exactly as planned. Building in extra time

around certain tasks is a smart strategy that helps you be prepared for the unexpected.
- **Be flexible about it.** Even if you try all these great tips, be prepared to have your schedule blown up to bits. When all else fails, throw your arms up and laugh! Being flexible and open to change saves you so much heartache. Of course, the terrific schedule you made can be destroyed at a moment's notice. Relax and "reschedule." It will all get done at the right time.

The almighty schedule is truly a self-care tool for caregivers when you use it as such. How, what, and when you schedule, if you are careful and thoughtful about it, can help you and those you care for stay calm while you get things done. Defining what is important when you schedule by how much comfort and ease you can build in is the trick to it all. In other words, schedule with love and concern for all involved.

Create a Calming Environment

Everyone enjoys being in a space that's soothing and calm. Creating an environment that's pleasant and feels good to be in doesn't take a lot of time or money. Even the busiest caregiver can take the time to add little touches to the rooms they spend the most time in. Here are a few things to help you create a pleasant space.

- **Buy some fresh flowers and make it a habit.** If the budget is too tight, drop hints to family and friends that flowers are always welcome to cheer the house up. They will love that they can get you something to help you in your caregiving. Adding holiday decorations to the mix is a great pick-me-up too!
- **Candles are always a lovely way to create an atmosphere of relaxation and pleasant aromas.** This can be another hint to give family and friends as a gift idea for you. If a lighted candle is not safe around those you care for, a deodorizer that emits a subtle scent is a good substitute. Find a scent that works to soothe and relax, like lavender or rosemary.
- **Consider the lighting.** It's all about the lighting. Don't subject yourself to harsh light. Soft, warm lighting makes a room comfy. You don't need new lamps, just new soft light bulbs. Sunlight is always best, but in the winter months or if those you care for are irritated by sunlight, soft, warm lighting creates a nice mood.

These little ways of creating peace and calm where you live and work inspire self-care and appreciation.

Stick to Your Rituals

Rituals are so valuable in the caregiving world. They can provide an anchor for those you care for. Sameness and consistency help to make people feel safe and secure. It makes sense that all feels right with the world if the same things happen every day. There is so much less to worry about if things change as little as possible.

Rituals can ground caregivers as well. You also need an anchor in your life. When you stick to your rituals even for small self-care routines, you are setting yourself up to feel balanced, centered, and serene.

Create the space and time for routines that make you feel whole and organized. Everything from teeth cleaning to moisturizing your body or making a healthy drink counts as an opportunity to pamper yourself consistently.

Although it may feel easier and faster to jump up out of bed and throw clothes on, grab an easy lunch and eat it on the run, or just fall into bed at night after a long caregiver day, it's always healthier to take a few moments to set things up and take time for yourself.

Actively set up morning, midday, and evening routine plans for yourself. Carve out at least fifteen minutes at each interval during the day and fill those fifteen minutes with routines that make you feel abundant, healthy, self-appreciating, and centered. Your day will begin and end with balance and a feeling of self-worth when you follow your self-care rituals.

Establish Great Relationships

Caregivers meet and work with lots of people. As you know, it takes a village to care for someone, and you will have a multitude of personalities you interact with in a single day. This alone is stressful, not to mention exhausting. Making sure you negotiate the best outcome for yourself and your loved ones takes some doing. Your emotional intelligence comes in handy here as well as great communication skills.

Make sure to apply these tactics when interacting with anyone, especially people who hold the key to getting the best service and care for those you love.

- **Find common ground.** As unique as we all are, we all have things in common. Most people in the caregiving world have compassion and empathy, and it's those qualities we need to bring out in ourselves and others. Get to know the people you interact with and find something you can share or agree on. Bonding is important.
- **Be open and honest.** Don't hide your concern about your loved one. Let people know how you feel and what's going on so they can understand that if you seem tense it's not about them. People are more willing to engage with open, honest, and authentic caregivers.
- **When you are in conversation with someone, listen to them.** You don't have to have the last word or say the right thing or rush to make your point. Let them give you feedback and be open to what they are saying. Everyone wants to be heard, and if you communicate that you are hearing them, the entire conversation takes a turn for the better.
- **Smile.** No matter how freaked out you are about what's happening with those you care for, smile, especially when approaching someone. We all feel better when someone comes up to us with a smile. It starts everything off on the right foot, and you have their attention in a positive way right from

the beginning. Everyone is stressed out in the caregiver world, and a smile has the magical ability to soften everything.

- **Be kind.** Even when doing something as simple as picking up medications at the pharmacy, if you take the time to be kind and pleasant, you establish rapport, which will reap rewards in the future. Being nice instead of nasty goes a long way in the caregiving space. Everyone has a lot to be uptight about, so dealing with someone warm and friendly is a godsend. If more people understood that you get more bees with honey, they would be more careful about how they act and how they approach others. Being warm and friendly get lots of appreciation and is usually returned in kind.

Establishing great relationships is such a powerful self-care tool for caregivers. When you maintain good relationships with people, you can count on them to be there when you need them. Being kind, pleasant, and caring is not only the right thing to do; it's the smart thing to do.

Get an Action Partner

Even though some caregivers may want to work alone, finding and working in tandem with an action partner can be a terrific way to get things done and clear away the procrastination around actions that feel like drudgery. It's also a great way for caregivers to connect with other people and socialize. This is a terrific way for caregivers to avoid isolation and build confidence.

An action partner is someone you check in with on a regular basis, sharing what you want to accomplish and then checking back in with them once the task or tasks are completed. These are called **bookending** actions, and they are a great way to stay accountable to someone else, so you have more incentive to take the actions or accomplish the task.

You can call, text, or email your action partner and exchange actions you want to take. You can start small and begin with one action and build from there. Doing this daily or weekly or even as the need arises will give you amazing results. You will be surprised how fulfilling it is to give and receive accountability, support, and encouragement.

When seeking possible action partners, it would be ideal if they were also caregivers since there would be so many compatible and familiar actions and tasks, but anyone who will consistently show up and work with you is a perfect candidate.

Tackle those uncomfortable caregiver actions you have been avoiding and get them done with the help of an action partner.

Build a Team

Caregiving takes a village. It is not a solo career. Putting a supportive caregiving team in place to work with you is critical. Your team will support you and enable you to be a better caregiver.

When putting this team together, it's important to know their availability and what they are willing and able to do. Ask them to be specific. Be honest and realistic about the gaps in your ability to juggle everything so you know where they can jump in to help.

Be clear on how much and how often they can pitch in. Make a list of chores, errands, small and big jobs, and times and places you could use help. Distribute this list and have them sign up. Remind them that as things change, their contribution may need to change, and you will keep them in the loop.

Make it easy for your team members to help you. Communicate with them often, use a schedule that everyone has access to, and keep it updated. There are great apps available for caregiver teams that allow everyone to see what's needed and sign up for tasks. Have them check in and confirm their commitments to you with a text or quick call.

Get over any trepidation, guilt, or embarrassment that you need help and are asking for it. The people that love you don't want to wait on the sidelines watching. They want to help you, and you must graciously let them. It's good for all of you!

Create a Budget

It may be necessary to manage the finances of those you care for. Caregivers can control expenditures, make sure the checkbook is balanced, and ensure that those they serve stay within the budget they can afford.

While you are at it, you should create a budget and spending plan for yourself, so you can track the expenses you incur as your caregiving role unfolds. This important and necessary tactic can save time and money and prevent overspending and accumulating debt.

Many caregivers will think nothing of buying extra little things for those they care for, such as additional groceries or better medical equipment, and these expenses can add up fast. Before they know what happened, caregivers can't pay their own expenses!

Create a budget and a spending plan for your own income and expenses. Be realistic and honest about what you need monthly to pay bills and add some extra cash for you to spend for fun. Once that's completed, see if there is money left over. If there is, this is the amount you can spend on those you care for. Be careful to stick to this amount and keep track of it in a separate caregiving account.

By keeping track of how much you have, and what you can spend on those you care for, you will make wise buying choices and not go into debt.

Wait Twenty-Four Hours

If you are faced with a situation where an injustice or critical mishap might affect your loved one and you feel highly charged emotions rise up in a reaction, it might be wise to step back a moment before exploding or going after whoever or whatever is responsible. To prevent yourself from going emotionally overboard and overreacting, there is a golden rule that caregivers can follow. Use restraint of pen and tongue, which means waiting at least twenty-four hours to respond or report whenever possible if there is no immediate danger to your loved one. Wait, if you have the luxury.

The minute you feel you are about to boil over and shout or send an angry email, do an about-face and zip your lips, close the email or text, and wait until tomorrow to send, discuss, or call.

Waiting twenty-four hours to give the doctor, nurse, facility, aide, or whoever it may be a piece of your mind allows you to calm down, get perspective, and be professional.

Sleep On It

Caregivers, because they often have to act quickly and decisively, can get uncomfortable hesitating about an issue. Getting things done quickly often gives a sense of relief. After all, the faster things get taken off your plates, the easier it is to spin them!

Not everything can be handled this way, however. Caregivers are confronted with important decisions daily, and some of those decisions need time and consideration. It's usually wise to permit yourself to mull over decisions that create major changes for those you care for or impact your caregiving role when you have the luxury to do so. Sometimes it's good to sleep on it.

When feasible, it's okay to put off a big decision or one that you are concerned with or confused by. Your brain is a capable computer, and it will run in the background to answer the question or fix the problem. You are allowed to take the space and time to just let the decision rest. Don't go over and over the pros and cons incessantly; just acknowledge that you will figure it out in the morning and trust yourself.

Sleeping on a decision is a good idea because you are usually overloaded by the end of the day, and it can be difficult to think clearly. Trusting that you can and do have the answers and will make the right decision at the right time, you can let it go and get some rest.

Know Your Limitations

Caregivers depend on their ability to handle and manage an extensive array of caregiving issues and problems. Even in the most difficult caregiving scenarios, caregivers are multitasking powerhouses with extraordinary abilities and skills.

Of all the skills needed to be a successful caregiver, one stands out, even though it's often overlooked, as a powerful tool to achieve that success. It's the ability to know your limitations.

Once you uncover and acknowledge your limitations, the pressure you put on yourself to be all things to all people quickly fades away. You don't have to be responsible for everything, only those things you handle well. The things beyond your scope and comfort zone can be delegated to others with different talents.

Getting to know your limitations takes honesty and objectivity. Be on the lookout for areas where you feel overwhelmed or stressed as you are caregiving. These can be duties or circumstances that feel too challenging or upsetting. If you are overreaching to complete or cope with certain things, it's time to admit that they may be too much for you. This is not defeat; it's delegation!

You can always ask your family and friends if they see you struggling in certain areas and want to help. Their supportive and honest opinions can help you decide what you can let go of and what you can keep. Knowing your limitations is a brilliant way to end up doing what you do best and then letting others shine as well.

Listen and Win

Everyone wants to be heard. When you listen closely to those you care for, you stay in tune with them and can stay in touch with their condition, progress, and mood. This is so valuable, as it cuts down the element of surprise. By listening and staying in touch, you can tailor your caregiving to meet their needs. Here are some great tips to up your listening game for winning results.

- **When you ask a question, actually listen to the answer.** Let go of your need to have the last word or put in your two cents, and concentrate on what your loved one, or the nurse, or the representative on the phone is trying to say. If they are not clear, don't get annoyed, get curious. Ask in order to learn and listen, not to give your opinion.
- **If your loved ones can't articulate or don't have the words they need, do not assume they have nothing to say.** Not all communication comes in the form of spoken words. Check their body language, the expression on their face, their gestures, and their state of being. What might they be trying to tell you? Being a good listener takes patience, creativity, and an honest attempt to understand someone even if they are having trouble explaining themselves.

We all want to be heard. When you let others know you are hearing them, the conversation can be joyful and informative, even if it's unusual and without words.

Stop Isolation by Socializing

Caregivers often get so caught up in the isolating world of caregiving that they lose contact with family and friends. They stop returning calls or texts, and start to lose touch.

Don't let this happen to you. Don't get so caught up in caring for others that you end up feeling alone. Socializing is one of the most important self-care actions caregivers can take to stay nurtured and grounded. We are built to have connection with others.

It's hard when you are too busy to answer calls or texts, so you probably ignore most of the attempts. Rather than try to balance socializing and interaction on the fly, schedule a time at least once a week to hang out with your tribe, family, or friends. Give them times you promise to be available and let them organize it. Do not miss this scheduled time. Do whatever you need to do to carve out this time, including finding someone to take over your caregiving duties so you can have uninterrupted time with the gang or other caregivers.

Let everyone know why it's so hard to reach you sometimes and suggest the best possible times to get a few minutes with you. Tell them to keep trying and that it means a lot to you to connect with them, that being in touch is very important to you. When you socialize, you honor the part of you that craves connection, so do it and do it often.

Handle Legal Documents

The often urgent nature of the caregiving experience causes you to prioritize the issues you have to deal with. The physical needs of those you care for must be addressed as quickly as possible, and getting everything stabilized can overshadow everything else. Once that is accomplished, one of the most important practical matters that needs attention is the completion of any legal documents that provide for your loved one's care in the future.

These documents ensure that the needs and wants of those in your care are clear and defined and that their rights and yours are protected. The importance of these documents cannot be stressed enough. Putting off dealing with these documents can have serious consequences down the road.

These documents allow those you care for to appoint a designated person to make decisions for them if they become incapacitated. The best time to set up these documents is when everyone is healthy and able to make decisions. Take care of this legal housekeeping as soon as it is possible and practical to do so.

Every state and country has different rules and regulations, so check with your local officials. Not all forms need to be completed by a lawyer, although it may be best if you consult a lawyer regarding financial forms and directives. Since everyone's situation is different, it may be wise to consult with a lawyer and have them draw up the documents required to address the unique needs of those you love and care for.

Here is a list of documents every caregiver should have in their arsenal so all situations are defined and directed:

- **A living will or an advanced directive** allows your loved one to state their wishes about end-of-life treatment. This will clarify which treatments they want and which they do not want, should they be unable to make those decisions at the time.

- **A healthcare proxy (or durable power of attorney)** is a document that allows your loved one to appoint a designated person to make medical decisions for them if they become incapacitated.
- **A HIPAA document** grants permission for a designated person to gain access to healthcare information that is usually only released to the patient. This allows the caregiver to have medical and insurance information released to them as the patient's representative.
- **A power of attorney** allows someone to appoint a designated person to make legal and financial decisions for them if they are unable to do so.
- **A last will and testament** designates how the assets and possessions of the deceased are to be distributed.

If possible, hold a family meeting to discuss and establish a plan of action to have all of this paperwork drawn up, signed, and on record. The heartache this can save down the road is immeasurable. Having all your document ducks in a row is the most caring thing you can do for those you love and for yourself.

Don't Argue, Don't Correct

Avoiding any type of confrontation with loved ones is pretty much at the top of any caregiver's agenda. There are so many difficult and scary challenges to be faced by both caregivers and those they care for that no one wants to be at odds with each other. It's counterproductive. The smoother the ride, the more comfortable everyone involved is.

No one wants to engage in spats or disagreements, but even the most balanced and patient caregivers can paint themselves into a corner by not being careful about what they say and how they handle communication with their loved ones.

People with dementia, Alzheimer's, and other forms of cognitive impairment are especially sensitive when communicating. Paying close attention to their needs and sensibilities is important. To make sure the conversations you have with those you love and care for are as gentle and rewarding as possible, use the following two strategies consistently. They will leave you both feeling a lot happier.

- **Don't argue with them.** It sounds like such a simple tactic, but it can be harder than you think, especially when you know they are wrong, and it may be about an important issue you need them to agree to. Getting them to agree may take a lot of negotiation, little white lies, and even some trickery, but flat-out arguing is useless and unkind. They may even be trying to argue out of a need to assert some power over something since they are losing control over so many things. Try to remember this and pull out all the patience you can muster and all the humor you can spare, but do not argue with them.
- **Do not correct them.** This, too, will be difficult, perhaps even harder than not arguing. No caregiver wants to accept that someone they love is becoming forgetful or is slipping away. As their disease progresses or they

begin to fail, their perceptions change, and their memories may shift and abandon them, leaving false narratives or mixed-up stories. Asking "Don't you remember?" or correcting them can be an unconscious attempt to try to change the reality of what's happening even if it's not intentional. There's no need to correct them; it doesn't change anything. Letting them see it their way or remember it the way they want or need to causes no harm. It's a gentle gesture of love to just let them discuss it the way they wish. You will avoid upsetting or hurting them. You can always change the subject or distract them with something else if it's upsetting to you. It will soon become second nature to just go along with their version of life since it pleases them and gives them comfort.

These two strategies are less upsetting and easier when you are practicing all your other self-care priorities so that you are balanced, rested, and calm and therefore have the bandwidth to be kind, understanding, and compassionate. When grounded, you have no need to argue or correct.

Manage a Crisis

You woke up ready for the day with your action plan, the intentions you wrote down the night before, and your schedule to follow. You were all ready to go and had expectations for an organized, smooth caregiving day. Then all hell broke loose. A health emergency erupts, important appointments get canceled, your loved one experiences a fall, or health insurance suddenly refuses to pay for an extremely expensive and necessary procedure. This sets the stage for catastrophe, and everything feels like it's falling apart.

All caregivers will face a crisis at least once in their caregiving journey. Falls or injuries, drastic changes in health, or unexpected legal or medical procedures create unforeseen challenges and put you in emergency mode.

When confronted with a crisis, try following this system of activities to help you get organized and grounded to meet the challenge in the most effective way possible.

1. To begin with, slow yourself down. This may sound counterintuitive, but it helps to slow everything down a bit so you can process and get coordinated. When you need to take immediate action and make that 911 call or stop the bleeding or get the healthcare provider on the phone, you need to move forward quickly. Take all the actions you need, but do so in a more calculated, precise, and settled manner than a frantic one.

2. It helps to take some long, deep breaths. Breathe deeply in through your nose for a count of 4, hold your breath for a count of 4, then slowly breathe out to a count of 4. This is taught to military personnel as a tool to calm down under

duress in combat. You can do this while you are taking stock of the situation or the actions needed to stabilize the situation. Your body and brain need to work together to concentrate and focus on the best plan of action, and by centering yourself you are better equipped to make the best decisions and take the appropriate actions.

3. Now that you have slowed down, have done your breathing exercise, and are a bit more collected, take stock and appraise the damage to see what you are truly dealing with. You might still be shaking and scared, but the next right thing you need to do will come to you. Begin to come up with your options and how to facilitate them. Write them down if that helps you.

4. Reach out and get help. Let your team know what's going on and how they can help you. Delegate when you can so your energy is focused on what matters.

Above all, trust yourself and your gut to know what to do and how to do it. You have been prepping for this the entire time you have been caregiving, and you have all the smarts and determination to see this through. Crises can test and frighten you, but the care you show those you love will see you through all of it.

Deal With the Aftereffects of a Crisis

A crisis can leave you feeling drained, depleted, and shell-shocked. By proactively working to recover and recharge from a crisis, the discomfort afterward can be reduced and a desired healthy balance can be restored much more quickly.

Once you have gallantly faced a crisis and are successfully on the other side of it, the same system of activities you used to cope with and manage the crisis can be used to cool down from and process the crisis once it has passed.

Here are some actions you can take after you are on the other side of crisis mode.

- Now that the emergency is over, take a minute, an hour, a day, or any amount of time you feel is necessary to recoup by slowing down. You have just been physically, emotionally, and spiritually distressed. You can now stop running around. Go slow with everything and relish having the time to sit back and relax a little. The crisis is over now; begin the process of letting the crisis go.
- While you don't need combat breathing to center your body now, you do need to establish calm and balance and let all that adrenaline that is still racing through your body play itself out. Deep breathing can help settle you down and replenish your body. Take some time to sit quietly, concentrate on your breathing, and let all the worry and fear dissipate.
- While it doesn't pay to go over and over the crisis, it is helpful to objectively take stock of what occurred and what you are now left with. When you are recuperated and ready, get clear about what the situation has created in terms of adjustments that need

to be made or changes that it caused. By taking a practical inventory of what happened and why, you can start to think about ways to compensate or how to move forward. Every crisis or emergency brings lessons and wisdom. Reflect on what this has taught you and how it will improve your knowledge and make you a better caregiver.

- This is a great time to meet with or talk to your team and get their impressions and input and share stories and impressions about what happened. Everyone will feel better by discussing what happened and how they feel about it. This helps to shake off any lasting upset or worry. Sharing your experience clarifies it and takes the bite out of it.

Reward yourself for a job well done. You showed up and stood up. You had grace under pressure. Do something nice for yourself. Give yourself lots of love and credit for an outstanding job combating an upsetting circumstance. You have been knocked sideways and are still standing. No matter what the outcome, you gave it your all and that is the greatest success.

Printed in Great Britain
by Amazon